# MARCO POLO

CS0029

D0547609

## Insider Tips

# DUBLIN

Glasgow

IRELAND

Dublin

UNITED
KINGDOM

*North
Sea*

Amsterdam

NETHER-
LANDS

*ATLANTIC
OCEAN*

London

Brussels

BELGIUM

*English Channel*

Paris

FRANCE

**www.marco-polo.com**

The best Insider Tips → p. 4

INSIDER TIP

Best of ... → p. 6

Sightseeing → p. 26

Food & Drink → p. 52

### SYMBOLS

**INSIDER TIP**   Insider Tip

★   Highlight

●●●●   Best of ...

☼   Scenic view

☺ Responsible travel: fair
trade principles and the
environment respected

(*) Telephone numbers that
are not toll-free

### PRICE CATEGORIES
### HOTELS

| | |
|---|---|
| *Expensive* | over 150 euro |
| *Moderate* | 100–150 euro |
| *Budget* | under 100 euro |

The prices are for a double
room per night including
breakfast

### PRICE CATEGORIES
### RESTAURANTS

| | |
|---|---|
| *Expensive* | over 35 euro |
| *Moderate* | 25–35 euro |
| *Budget* | under 25 euro |

The prices are for a three-
course meal without drinks

On the cover: Kilmainham Gaol: death for freedom's sake p. 50 | Great live music in The Cobblestone p. 73

# CONTENTS

Shopping → p. 62

Entertainment → p. 70

Where to stay → p. 78

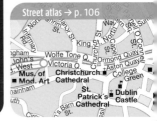
Street atlas → p. 106

## DID YOU KNOW?

## MAPS IN THE GUIDEBOOK

(108 A1) Page numbers and coordinates refer to the street atlas
Map of surrounding area on p. 116/117
(0) Site/address located off the map. Coordinates are also given for places that are not marked on the street atlas. A public transportation map and a map of the Temple Bar district inside the back cover

## INSIDE BACK COVER: PULL-OUT MAP →

## PULL-OUT MAP 𝄞

(𝄞 A–B 2–3) Refers to the removable pull-out map

# The best
# MARCO POLO
# Insider Tips

## Our top 15 Insider Tips

INSIDER **TIP** **Beautiful interior**

The *Dublin Writers Museum* is in a beautiful restored Georgian building and if you visit its café or the affiliated bookstore you won't have to pay an entrance fee to the museum → **p. 43**

INSIDER **TIP** **Satisfy your fashion desires**

You can't afford top international designers like Galliano and company? No problem – hire your dream designer outfit from *Covet – The Borrowers Boudoir* → **p. 66**

INSIDER **TIP** **The expert's choice**

Museum curators display and discuss their favourite pieces in the *Curator's Room* at the National Museum – Decorative Arts → **p. 45**

INSIDER **TIP** **Where Irish roughnecks meet**

A live hurling match or a rowdy Gaelic football game at *Croke Park* will certainly be an experience to remember (photo above) → **p. 20**

INSIDER **TIP** **Choir music at church**

The acclaimed *Palestrina Choir* sings every Sunday at the eleven o'clock mass at the Roman Catholic St Mary's Pro-Cathedral → **p. 47**

INSIDER **TIP** **Getting to know the city, bite by bite**

On the *Dublin Tasting Trail* you can do some unusual sightseeing when you visit local fresh markets, fishmongers and cheese specialists with plenty delicious food to taste along the way – you will not go hungry on this tour → **p. 103**

INSIDER **TIP** **Where the Dubliners pray**

The lavish *Augustinian Church* is the parish church for the residents of the Liberties suburb of the city and is a neo-Gothic jewel → **p. 48**

INSIDER **TIP** **Ease up on the credit card**

A great way to save money is to take advantage of some of Dublin's excellent pre-theatre *set menus* → **p. 52**

**INSIDER TIP** Stylish bar

Don't be put off by the entrance – the *Market Bar* is one of Dublin's most stylish venues – have a delicious coffee during the day or a fine wine in the evening → **p. 61**

**INSIDER TIP** The Backroom

There is no secret gambling in The Backroom at Cobblestone – as one might suspect from looking at the name – instead it plays host to famous and up-and-coming *live bands* → **p. 73**

**INSIDER TIP** One for all

Whether vegetarian or meat lover: at *Louie's Bistro* everyone enjoys the relaxed atmosphere and delicious fare in this beautifully restored Georgian restaurant. They also have a pre-7pm early bird special → **p. 61**

**INSIDER TIP** Bus ride with panoramic views

For a splendid ocean view take the bus *route 31 B* along the coast to the fishing village of Howth → **p. 51**

**INSIDER TIP** An alternative to Guinness

If you only ever drink the famous black in Dublin, you will be missing out. The *Porterhouse* pub has their own in-house micro-brewery so they have their own top quality and tasty beer on tap → **p. 76**

**INSIDER TIP** Fine ingredients for a picnic

Fashion above, food below: at the *Avocas Food Hall* they have both beautiful clothing and some extremely delicious goodies on offer. Freshly baked bread, Irish cheese and tasty pies, all perfect for a marvellous picnic on St Stephen's Green just around the corner (photo below) →**p. 66**

**INSIDER TIP** Peaceful hostel for the hungry

A bit more peaceful than other hostels, Internet access and garden – but the biggest bonus at the *Globetrotters* hostel is their lavish Irish breakfast → **p. 84**

# BEST OF ...

**FOR FREE**

● **Wide view across the city**
If you want to see Dublin from above, you'll have to pay: for the Dublin Wheel or the Chimney but the view from *Howth Heath* over the Dublin Bay, the mountains and many other parts of the city is free and peaceful. The short ascent begins behind the Deer Park Hotel → p. 80

● **Cinema under the stars**
A visit to the movies could well diminish your dinner budget so if you would like to have both then go to the *Meeting House Square* in the Temple Bar. On Saturdays in summer they show classic movies outside for free → p. 74

● **An ecologically friendly option**
If your feet hurt from all the sightseeing, then why not let the comfortable and eco-friendly *Ecocab* take you anywhere within Dublin's city centre. The rickshaw-like tricycles are a free service, thanks to corporate sponsorship (photo) → p. 103

● **A long night of Dublin culture**
Dublin has followed the same trend as other European capitals and holds a *Culture Night* every September. The entire city joins in with music, art, readings, and workshops until dawn, museums, theatres, pubs ... and best of all is that everything is for free → p. 95

● **Celtic gold – still for free**
Despite the economic crisis, the entrance to state museums is still free. Visit the *National Museum* and admire the precious collection with exhibits from the Viking and a gold collection from the prosperous days of the Celtic tribes → p. 33

● **Live music at the pub**
The cost of tickets for live concerts can quickly dent your wallet but that is not the case in Dublin. There are still pubs here where you can enjoy live Irish music for free. Good venues are *The Brazen Head* and *Hughes' Bar* → p. 73, 74

◐◐◐◐ Dots in guidebook refer to 'Best of ...' tips

● *Dublin's poets and the thirst*
If you would like to follow in the footsteps of poets, you need not worry about getting thirsty on the way. On the *Literary Pub Crawl* actors lead you from pub to pub and as they go along they recite verses, sing ballads, act out melodramas and talk about the authors' works → p. 103

● *The Georgian style Merrion Square*
The brightly coloured doors of the *Merrion Square*, built in Georgian style, will make quite an impression on you. In the middle of the beautiful park there is a collection of historic street lamps and a few sculptures, one of Oscar Wilde, who lived at no. 1 (photo) between 1855 and 1876 → p. 31

● *The rich and famous*
If you want to keep an eye out for celebrities, the best place to go is the *Horseshoe Bar* at the Shelbourne Hotel. This is the place to see and be seen and the hotel and its bar are a Dublin institution, quite a few scandals have played out here → p. 81

● *Cultural market*
Dive into the multiculturalism of *Moore Street*: no other street better symbolises the old and the new Dublin. The garrulous women at this market are an Irish institution but they now have new neighbours: immigrants from Africa, Asia and Eastern Europe have opened grocery stores, hair salons, music shops and a pub → p. 65

● *Favourite number game*
Nowhere is Ireland more Irish than at bingo. The lottery game was first introduced by the Catholic Church as a fundraiser. Bingo evenings take place in the community halls and at the *National Stadium*. Try your luck! → p. 72

● *Train trip along the coast*
Get to know Ireland starting from Dublin: the *Dart* (Dublin Area Rapid Transport) will take you once around Dublin Bay. The commuter train goes from Howth and Malahide in the north of Dublin along the coast up to Greystones in county Wicklow → p. 51, 102

ONLY IN

# BEST OF ...

**RAIN**

● *For a pint*
*Mulligan's* pub – which dates back to 1732 – has been renovated with great care so that you can still drink your beer in an authentic and cosy atmosphere → **p. 75**

● *Grown under glass*
The original Victorian *greenhouses* in the 200-year-old botanical garden are exceptional. Stroll between the palms and orchids under the remarkable curvilinear glass ceiling and shelter from the rain → **p. 50**

● *Behind the prison gates*
The *Kilmainham Gaol* in western Dublin is Ireland's Bastille. Walking through the dark building gives you a crash course in Irish history: from 1796–1924 the prison was full of Irish rebels who fought against the British occupation (photo) → **p. 50**

● *Eat from the packet*
Visit Ireland's most famous chipper: *Leo Burdock's Fish and Chips Shop*. It has been going strong since 1913 and has served their famous battered fried fish to a long list of celebrities from Mick Jagger to Tom Cruise and Edith Piaf. Crispy goodness in a paper bag! → **p. 60**

● *All about leprechauns*
Dive into Irish mythology in the *Leprechaun Museum*. The museum's twelve interactive chapters take you through the history of the leprechaun – from the first sighting in the 8th century right through to today's representation in films and pop music → **p. 92**

● *In the world of film*
Three in one: the *Irish Film Institute* has a cinema – usually showing an interesting selection of movies – a very affordable café and a well organised DVD shop → **p. 73**

# RELAX AND CHILL OUT
## Take it easy and spoil yourself

● **Wellness with spring water**
The *Wells Spa* at the Hotel Brook Lodge only uses its own well water for their mud baths, massages and aromatherapy. If you are up to it, you can also take a very revitalising ice shower after one of your treatments → **p. 37**

● **A sanctuary of green**
Uncomplicated and free of charge, you can relax in *Phoenix Park*, one of the largest inner-city parkland areas in the world. Covering an area of more than 1752 acres, there is more than enough space for a quiet picnic or an afternoon nap in the sun (photo) → **p. 50**

● **Massaged from head to toe**
Aches and pains do not stand a chance: three qualified therapists offer traditional Thai massages – oil massages, foot massages, shoulder and back massages as well as Indian head massages – at the *Mai Thai Massage* in the heart of the Temple Bar → **p. 37**

● **Getting the body into top form**
At *Therapie* your body will be whipped into fantastic form with a myriad of different treatments. Laser hair removal, specialist anti-wrinkle skin care treatments, beauty massages as well as laser-eye treatments are all on offer and they even have a slimming tea → **p. 37**

● **Unwind to church music**
Even for non-believers a service in a Catholic cathedral can be very relaxing – especially on Sunday mornings when the magnificent *Palestrina Choir* sings the mass at St Mary's Pro-Cathedral → **p. 47**

● **Meditate on the masterpiece**
Michelangelo Caravaggio's painting 'The Taking of Christ' is the most significant exhibit at the *National Gallery*. Avoid the busy weekend opening times and spend a weekday relaxing on the padded seat in front of the painting and meditate on it for hours → **p. 32**

INTRODUCTION

# DISCOVER DUBLIN!

James Joyce wrote that his hometown was 'more beautiful naturally in my opinion than what I have seen of England, Switzerland, France, Austria, or Italy'. With his epic novel, 'Ulysses', he created a literary monument that no other city has so far been able to claim. In Gaelic the Irish capital is known as *Baile Átha Cliath,* the 'town of the hurdled ford' and its Anglicised name also originated from the Gaelic: *Dubhlinn* means 'black pool' and describes the basin area filled with dark water which formed where the rivers Liffey and Poddle (today an underground river) met and where the historic city settlement began.

The Irish capital is rich with museums and galleries, churches and sport facilities, with sightseeing attractions, shopping opportunities and concert halls, with cinemas and theatres, but most of all – with pubs! Almost everything is within easy walking distance, as the city centre is small. It is bordered in the north by the Royal Canal and in the south by the Grand Canal and its suburbs stretch out to the north, south and west of the centre.

Photo: View over the Liffey in Dublin's city centre

Dublin is a youthful city with almost a third of its population under 25 years of age and the youth have given the city its vibrant rhythm and atmosphere and alongside the lovely old pubs are now chic modern bars and trendy clubs. Temple Bar – an area that was earmarked for a bus terminal– was instead converted into an entertainment district, where the youth hang out at weekends until late at night. The local gastronomy also underwent a revolution and the traditional Irish home style cuisine has taken on some influences from international cuisines from all over the world. No city in Europe has seen as much change as Dublin has in the past 20 years.

## From Europe's poorhouse to one of the richest countries ...

The Dubliners have also had a lot of experience with harsh economic and political upheavals which run like a thread through the Irish capital's history. The Vikings founded the settlement on the Liffey around 841, but were conquered by Irish King Brian Boru in 1014 and assimilated into the Celtic population. From 1170 Dublin was ruled by the British kings and was a dependent trade and government centre in the high Middle Ages. From Dublin Castle the British Crown set out to subjugate Ireland, which they finally managed to do after the Reformation. This began the era of Protestant reign over a predominantly Catholic country. After the turmoil of the Reformation, and the wars of the mid 1700s, Dublin finally experienced a time of peace and prosperity in 1690. The narrow, impoverished alleyways of the Middle Ages gave way to broad streets and elegant squares lined with prosperous Georgian townhouses and buildings.

The Sean O'Casey Bridge leads directly into the Docklands – Dublin's boomtown in the 1990s

After the dissolution of the Irish parliament in 1801 Dublin lost its political and social significance but in the 20th century the Irish patriots fight for independence finally came to bore fruit. A key event was the Easter Rising in 1916 when fierce fighting took place all over Dublin, especially at the central post office at O'Connell Street. It was only with the establishment of the independent Irish state in 1921 that Dublin finally became the capital city.

Since the 1990s the Emerald Isle has undergone a dramatic upheaval, a roller coaster ride from the poorhouse of Europe to one of the richest countries in the world – and back to being the poorhouse. In 1987 the country experienced an economic boom unequalled anywhere else in Europe. This came about as a result of a social pact between the country's unions, employers and the state in which they agreed on reductions in taxes but only minimal salary increases. At the same time multinational companies were attracted to the country by its low taxes and ready-to-use factories. The average income rose by 60 per cent and unemployment was practically unheard of.

The economic boom and the consequent social changes arrived suddenly in Ireland and the country's transformation meant that the economy became known as the 'Celtic tiger'. The boom was most evident

> ... in the world and back to being a poorhouse

in Dublin. The inner city's fallow areas were renwed with the construction of modern building complexes. The suburb of Smithfield, a working class district with narrow alleys and brick houses, was transformed. The place was given new cobblestone

streets and modern street lamps, and on the massive site of an old whiskey distillery, a new world was born: *Smithfield Village* with luxury hotels, shopping arcade, Thai restaurant, 200 apartments and an observation tower (the chimney of the old distillery) with a glass lift. Or the Liffey: for hundreds of years the river was neglected and used as a rubbish tip, the buildings along its banks slid into decay and residents moved away. The urban revival saw the river transformed with a promenade, wooden boardwalks and a pedestrian bridge and now, on National Day on 17 March, there is also a fireworks display over the river. And the largest development in Irish history got underway in the old harbour area where apartments, hotels, parks, a conference complex and a shopping centre were created in the new district known as the Docklands.

The economic boom also saw an influx of immigrants. In 1996 the number of immigrants exceeded the number of emigrants for the first time and after the new millennium more than 50,000 immigrants arrived per year. The population rose to over 4 million of which almost ten per cent were immigrants, the largest group being the Polish. Supermarkets introduced special sections for Polish produce and Dublin's evening paper, the 'Evening Herald', included an eight-page supplement every Friday in Polish with tips for immigrants. There were also arrivals from Nigeria, the Baltics and China.

Dublin has become colourful and cosmopolitan. There are no longer the uniform rows of grey shops with pale Irishmen but instead there are the immigrants with their exotic shops and restaurants, especially in the area around Parnell Street where there are now more than half a dozen (comparably cheap) Chinese restaurants. There are also Chinese and Afro-Caribbean supermarkets, where the locals also go shopping. Tucked amongst them is one establishment left over from the old days that sells parrots.

In Moore Street, a side street off Parnell Street, the old and the new Dublin sit side by side. This street, which is a pedestrian zone, is where fruit and vegetable traders – with the Irish gift of the gab – sell their produce from traditional wooden stalls as they have been doing for centuries. However, nowdays the rows of shops that line the street are in the hands of foreign folk: Nigerian and Chinese cafés, a hair salon with hair pieces for African women, a Caribbean supermarket. Even the butcher *FX Buckley's*, who has been running his business here for a hundred years, now sells pig heads and tongues which are not something the Irish eat but which are prized by the Chinese.

**Ghost towns: 300,000 houses stand empty**

The boom saw German, American, French, British and Swiss banks investing billions of euro into the Irish financial economy. The money flowed in primarily as credit for the construction boom driven in turn by the newly implemented tax reductions. However, by 2008 the entire economy came crashing down. The property bubble burst, the construction companies were unable to pay back their loans to the Irish banks, which in turn could not honour their debts with the international banks. About 300,000 houses now stand empty and there are hundreds of ghost towns.

The Irish government had to ask the European Union and the International Monetary Fund (IMF) for help and a rescue package was put in place but the conditions were brutal: a drastic savings programme and interest of almost six per cent. The consequences are dire: an unemployment rate that harks back to the 1980s, 1000 Irish emigrating every week, property values of homes have gone into free-fall and 75,000 people can no longer afford their mortgages. Many foreign workers have returned home and the houses they were renting in Dublin are now all standing empty. This downward economic spiral has meant that the once powerful Ireland is now saddled with a mountain of unpaid debt. The country is in danger of declaring bankruptcy.

None of this is really noticeable to the visiting holidaymaker, restaurant and hotel prices have dropped somewhat but Dublin is certainly not a cheap city. The heart of the city is (and always has been)

> **Dublin has on average less rainfall than Nice**

the area around the city's 400-year-old university, Trinity College, the chic shopping district around Grafton Street and the government district around Merrion Square and St Stephen's Green, whose beautiful parks are perfect for a lazy catnap, and there is way more space over in Phoenix Park, north-west of the centre, Europe's most extensive urban park.

In Dublin's busy O'Connell Street visitors experience little of the impact of the economic crisis

For literature fans Dublin is still a real paradise. In museums, theatres and on Bloomsday, the annual James Joyce Festival on 16 June, Dublin celebrates its writers and its literary heritage and the Irish love of storytelling and music also evidenced in their pubs. Here you will discover that pubs and culture are not a contradiction but instead complement each other and that they will round off your journey to Dublin beautifully.

The weather certainly has stayed exactly the same, which is a good thing because the constant rain has served to protect the island from mass tourism and hotel tower blocks. There is a saying that the Irish have two favourite days of year: Christmas and summer. This is an exaggeration as generations of holidaymakers have actually returned from Ireland with a suntan – it really is just a matter of luck – Dublin's annual rainfall is less than Nice's. The Irish also have another saying, 'A stranger is a friend you haven't met yet'. This is true of Dubliners so go there and meet them!

# WHAT'S HOT

## 1 Off to the Temple Bar

*Pasta pasta* The mother of all noodle bars is *Wagamama*. Here every conceivable kind of noodle is cut, twirled and slurped, be it rice or wheat, udon, soba or ramen *(South King St.)*. *Wagamama* paved the way for other cool noodle eateries like the *Diep Noodle Bar* which specialises in Vietnamese and Thai *(Mortons, Hatch St.)*. At *Café Mao* even the side dish to the chilli-lime beef (steamed noodles made with ginger, soya sauce and coriander) is a delight *(2–3 Chatham Row)*.

## Bring your own

## 2

*Goodbye wine list* Increasing numbers of restaurants now operate without a liquor licence. This means that guests can bring along their own wine. The *Seagrass* even forgoes a corkage fee with its international cuisine *(30 South Richmond St., photo)* while Moustafa Keshk serves delicious home style cooking at the *Keshk Café (129 Upper Leeson St.)*. You can select the wine for the oriental meal beforehand, like for example at the wine boutique *Louis Albrouze*. Here you can order the appropriate wine in advance so that your white is already chilled and the your red decanted *(127 Upper Lesson St.)*.

## 3 Emerald Isle

*Eco* Ride through Dublin – for free and without a carbon footprint – in a pedal-powered *EcoCab (www.ecocabs.ie, photo)*. Your route should also lead you to *Leaf Living*, where you can find everything from eco-friendly cleaning agents to birdsong clocks, whatever your green heart desires *(Whitefriar St.)*. Next up should be *Edun*, U2 singer Bono and his wife Ali Hewson's fair trade fashion label, where you can get items that are guaranteed to make you look good *(Brown Thomas & Co, Grafton St.)*.

# And now for a word

*The city of literature* Unesco have officially named Dublin as a 'City of Literature' and in so doing have further flamed the literary ambitions of its up-and-coming writers. Readings by its literary youth usually take place in comfortable relaxed environments like *Cassidy's Bar (27 Westmoreland St.)* or the indie bookstore *Chapters (Parnell St.)*. An overview of the new wave of writers can be found at *Dublin Book Festival (www.dublin bookfestival.com)*. One person who has succeeded is Roslyn Fuller (photo) a Canadian who is now a Dublin native, who made it on to the bestseller list with her debut 'ISAK' *(www. irishwritersexchange.com)*. If you have lost your heart to Irish literature, you will enjoy *Cathach Books* which specialises in Irish rarities and lesser known authors *(10 Duke St.)*.

# Pop-up spaces

*Art on the go* Empty factories, or shops, that are turned into a creative space. Eli McBett has taken over an old workshop and instead of an oil change there is now oil on canvas. The exhibitions at the *SHE-D* are constantly changing and are always worth seeing *(43 Gardiner Lane, www.mcbett.net, photo)*. To make spaces available to artists is also *Trans-Colonia's* goal, this artists' initiative keeps instigating exciting new projects *(http://sites. google.com/site/recycledspace)* while the *Workmans Club* has a proper (fixed) address where artists can work towards their breakthrough. It is also a venue for concerts, exhibitions and performances *(10 Wellington Quay)*.

# IN A NUTSHELL

## **B**LOOMSDAY

On the morning of 16 June 1904 Leopold Bloom, the 38-year-old protagonist of James Joyce's 'Ulysses', closed the door to his house in 7 Eccles Street, walked past Larry O'Rourke's pub and bought some kidneys at the Dlugaczs Butchery. On his way he mused, 'a good puzzle would be cross Dublin without passing a pub' and every year since 1954 James Joyce followers have been trying to do just so when, on the 16 June, they follow in Bloom's footsteps through the Irish capital. Some even arrive on Bloomsday in Edwardian outfits and many stops along Bloom's way, like the Sandycove defence tower, are still as they were in his day. Joyce spent five days there with the writer Oliver St John Gogarty and the Anglo-Irishman Samuel Trench. Even Sweny's Chemist Shop, where Bloom bought a bar of lemon soap, is still there, 'Chemists rarely move', Bloom correctly prophesied. This also applies to the dead in the Glasnevin Cemetery, where the novel's hero, and three other mourners, travelled to by carriage. Besides the streets and places that Bloom visited in the city on his walk (between eight in the morning and two at night) there are still many other shops and taverns which can be explored by the Joyce pilgrims. Bloom also stopped and had a gorgonzola sand-

---

Photo: In Ireland the pub is at the centre of social life

**What's the *craic*? Here you find all you need to know about shamrocks, linesmen in long white coats and King George's favourite doors**

wich and a glass of burgundy at Davy Byrne's and this meal is still served at Davy Byrne's, but only on Bloomsday.

# CRAIC

In Ireland the pub is the focus of life. It is much more than a just a place where you go to drink beer, rather it is a place that nurtures two very important elements of Irish culture: music and conversation. The importance of traditional music to the Irish (which still sounds the best when played in a pub) is well documented but even more important than the music is the conversation, as the Irish are a garrulous and humorous folk. Their eloquence has not only earned them the Nobel Prize for Literature but it is also something that comes in handy every evening at the bar counter. And where there is Irish talk there is Irish laughter and so you will often hear the word *craic*, which is roughly translated as 'fun'. 'What's the *craic*?' can mean, 'What's going on?' or 'What's up?' and as a question it can also be a challenge to tell an entertaining and humorous story. After a successful evening at the pub you say, 'It was great *craic*!' – 'We had a lot of fun!'

# GAELIC

Tourists in Dublin often wonder how many buses drive to *An Lár* as there is no mention of the place in conversation and it is not even recorded on the city map. *An Lár* is the Gaelic (Gaelic is the generic name for both Irish and Scottish but is the word used in Ireland for Irish) word for the city centre. In Ireland Irish is, according to the 1937 Constitution, the country's first language – English is only the second official language – however, the reality stands in stark contrast to this constitutional wish. Irish is a Celtic language that was allowed to flourish freely up until the 16th century when Henry VIII and his followers tried to suppress their rebellious Irish subjects by forcing English laws and language on to them. After the great famine in the mid 1900s it was forbidden to speak Irish at school. The children who did were forced to carry a wooden stick around their necks and for every Irish word they spoken, a mark was notched into the stick. Once a certain number of marks had been reached, the parents were forced to pay a fine. Only once the independence movement, towards the end of the 19th century, was underway was there a revival of the language and after independence in 1922 the new government began actively promoting the language. Gaelic was taught in schools and *Gaeltachts* – communities with Irish as a home language – were founded. Tax reductions and housing

# IRISH ROUGHNECKS

The Irish are a sports-mad, competitive nation, something that is very evident during a live match of either one of their traditional Irish sports of *hurling* (with women: *camogie*) or *Gaelic football*. The most important games of the *All Ireland Football Championship* take place between April and September and those of the *National Hurling League* between February and April at the *Croke Park Stadium* by the *Gaelic Athletic Association (Jones Road | northern suburb Drumcondra | tel. 018 36 32 22 | www.crokepark.ie)*. The highlight of the season is the all-Irish finals on the first and third Sunday in September, also in Croke Park. Game fixtures are listed on the Gaelic Athletic Association's website *(www.gaa.ie)*. Besides football, the Irish also love rugby. A highlight for rugby fans is the *Six Nations Championship (January–March)* between England, France, Ireland, Italy, Scotland and Wales. The old *Lansdowne Road Stadium*, which was built in 1832 in the southern suburb of Ballsbridge *(DART: Lansdowne Road | tel.01 6 68 46 01 | www.irish rugby.ie)* had to give way to the super modern 50,000 seater *Aviva Stadium*, which opened in 2010. Football is now also played there and it is where the Irish national football team play their home matches.

subsidies were used as incentives to encourage people to settle in these areas. Even in Dublin housing complexes were created specifically for Irish-speaking residents. Despite these efforts Irish Gaelic is a dying language. But there are still toilet signs that may create a little problem for harried tourists so do not make the assumption that *fir* means 'woman' and *mná* means 'man' or you may end up walking through the wrong door!

# GAELIC FOOTBALL

This traditional Irish sport is a distant cousin to both rugby and football. It also involves progressing the ball up field to score, either by shooting into the net (which scores three points) or over the H-shaped goal posts (a single point) but in this game hands are also allowed. Linesmen and umpires in long, white jackets oversee the game from the sidelines and signal a score with a flag wave. There are strict rules regarding behaviour on field, something which may not be immediately obvious to the inexperienced spectator. Another Gaelic game is hurling, a distant relative to hockey, but far more combative. Both of these sports were brought back to popularity towards the 19th century by the Gaelic Athletic Association (GAA) after centuries of suppression by the British. Sport and rebellion were interlinked right from the beginning as police, prison wardens and soldiers were all banned from becoming members of the GAA. GAA members on the other hand were not allowed to watch 'barbaric British sports like rugby, football or cricket much less partake in them and this continued right up until the 1950s. These days the association is a pillar of society with many players moving into politics, a prime example is Jack Lynch, the hurling star from Cork, who went on to become the prime minister

A **INSIDER TIP** visit to a Gaelic football or hurling match is guaranteed to be an unforgettable experience, the GAA league amateurs often play at the Croke Park Stadium (see box) in Dublin's Drumcondra suburb.

Very Georgian: Dublin Door

# GEORGIAN

Georgian architecture in Dublin dates from 1714–1830, where four consecutive British kings were called George. At the time Dublin was the second most important city (after London) in the emerging British trade empire and the city experienced a period of prosperity and growth. The population grew from 60,000 to 224,000 and affluent new suburbs developed. They had wide streets, elegant squares and prestigious residences and homes in a characteristically classical style. The most striking aspect of the Georgian architecture is its famous Dublin doorways. The doors are a decorative contrast to the simple brick façades which are generally only embellished with a small cast iron balcony on the first floor. The doors, on the other hand, draw the eye with lots of detail. Single or double columns frame the doors and above the door itself are ornamental semi-circular fanlight windows, which provide a view on to the stucco mouldings of the ceilings within. The doors themselves are all painted in bright, bold colours and there are rarely two adjacent homes with the same colour door. Highly polished brass fittings – knockers, knobs, letter slots, bells and nameplates – all complete the perfect image of the famous Georgian Dublin doors.

# GUINNESS

The pub is the Irishman's extended living room, and it actually developed from the living room. In the Middle Ages most Irish families brewed their own beer. Through word of mouth everyone soon got to know who produced the best beer in the neighbourhood, and those families then began to make a business out of selling their beer. In 1682 William Petty discovered that more than 1200 (out of 6025) homes in Dublin sold alcohol and it was from this practice that many of the breweries had their beginnings. One of them, which was rundown and dilapidated, was purchased by Arthur Guinness on 31 December 1759. With more than just a touch of optimism, the 34-year-old Protestant from Kildare paid a hundred pounds to lease the brewery for 9000 years for an annual rent of 45 pounds. His family thought he was crazy. The original building was a mere 4 acres, today it covers over 64 acres and is on both sides of Thomas Street. In the beginning, Arthur Guinness only brewed light beer and

English ale, and it was only later that he changed to the famous dark stout. In 1914 Guinness was the largest brewery in the world. Today the black stout is available in more than 150 countries. At the Dublin headquarters 4 million pints are produced daily. Many poets and writers were also quite preoccupied with Guinness, whether in a pub or in their works. Benjamin Disraeli, Graham Greene and Charles Dickens all wrote about it at some point or another and the mystery writer Dorothy L. Sayers kept it short and sweet when she said, 'Guinness is good for you', and that was also their first advertising slogan in 1929. The Guinness Book of Records, which was first published in 1955, is one of the top-selling books in the world after the Bible and the Koran. It was started after an argument between the Guinness Managing Director Hugh Beaver and a hunting friend. The contention was about which bird was the fastest in the world and the book was initially meant as an advertising stunt, but it was a commercial hit and is now so successful that it has an editorial department of 50 and appears in almost 40 different languages.

# HARP AND SHAMROCK

Two national symbols are ubiquitous in Dublin. The first is the twelve-stringed harp, which is a symbol for the bards and therefore music and literature. When the flag – with a yellow harp on a blue background – is raised in Phoenix Park it indicates that the head of state is at home, the state residence is right in the middle of the park. The harp is also seen as part of the stone coat of arms on the façades of some of the more prestigious buildings but it is most often seen as the Guinness logo. However, but the Guinness harp is inverted because in Ireland it would be presumptuous to depict a state harp on a glass of beer.

Another Irish symbol is the clover leaf, for botanists *trifolium dubium,* for the general population shamrock. On their National Day, St Patrick's Day (17 March), the nurseries do a booming trade as every patriotic Dubliner wears a green shamrock

Ireland in the 12th century, could not pronounce the word, they corrupted it to whiskey. Irish whiskey – previously it was written like the Scottish whisky without the 'e' – has been available for more than a thousand years. The Irish are proud that

Irish whiskey is produced according to the Purity Act and it has no additives

sprig in their buttonhole. Legend has it that St Patrick used the three-leafed clover during his missionary work in the 5th century to explain the teaching of the Holy Trinity. The shamrock symbol appears when Ireland hosts a special event, on the shirts of the Irish football and rugby teams or part of the logo for the tourism board.

# WHISKEY

Whiskey's name has its origins in the old Gaelic *Uisce Beatha*, which means 'water of life'. Because the soldiers of the British King Henry II, who occupied

they invented it, even though the Scots like to take credit for it. As proof, the Scots point out that there are far more Scottish brands than Irish, but the classic Irish comeback is that the reason for that is that the Scots are 'still practising'. Until the Prohibition, Irish whiskey dominated the market place in the United States. But during the prohibition from 1920–1933 many Americans made illegal moonshine whiskey and then labelled it with well-known Irish brand names which then gave Irish whiskeys a bad reputation. Once Prohibition was lifted, Scottish whisky dominated the American market.

# THE PERFECT DAY
## Dublin in 24 hours

**09:00am** **BETWEEN TEAROOMS AND COFFEE HOUSES**

A perfect day in Dublin begins with a breakfast at *Bewley's Café* → p. 54, in Grafton Street. Ernest Bewley opened his establishment in 1927 and drew his inspiration from the great Viennese coffee houses and from exotic Oriental tearooms. Bewley's has been carbon neutral since 2008 and the business ascribes to fair trade practices and sells organic products. Try the organic porridge or the delicious sweet pancakes, before you go on your way.

**10:00am** **MOLLY AND THE BOOK OF KELLS**

Now you go along Grafton Street in a northerly direction, past the *Molly Malone statue* → p. 36 (photo left), who sold fish by day and her body by night. On the right is the main entrance to the Trinity College with its old library and the magnificent *Book of Kells* → p. 37, which you must take time to view. Next is Dame Street, past the old parliament buildings and the modern central bank. Behind it is the entertainment district Temple Bar, but save this area for later ...

**12:00pm** **WHERE STARS GET THEIR FINGERS DIRTY**

At the end of Dame Street and its extension Lord Edward Street take a quick look at *Christ Church Cathedral* → p. 38, one of two Protestant cathedrals in Dublin. By now you are probably feeling hungry again. Opposite the cathedral, at the beginning of Werburgh Street, is *Leo Burdock's* → p. 60, the most famous chipper in Ireland. Mick Jagger, Rod Stewart, Tom Cruise, Bruce Springsteen and Edith Piaf have all had greasy fingers from eating Burdock's famous fish and chips.

**01:00pm** **CORPSES IN THE CRYPT**

Freshly fortified you continue on your trip: go past *Dublinia* → p. 40 and *St Audoen's Church* → p. 41, down Bridge Street. At the end, just before the Liffey, is the oldest pub in Dublin, *The Brazen Head* → p. 73, but it is still too early for a pint. Go further on to Father Matthew Bridge, pass Four Courts (photo right) on your left and along Church Street up to *St Michan's Church* → p. 47. This is worth a stop. Handel apparently played his 'Messiah' on the St Michan

# Get to know some of the most dazzling, exciting and relaxing facets of Dublin – all in a single day

organ. In the crypts under the church are some mummified corpses, some of which have been there for 800 years. The tannin-rich air of the cyrpts prevents their decay. It stands to reason that this place inspired Bram Stoker to create his Dracula.

## 03:00pm CHILD'S PLAY

Go back a few steps and turn left into Chancery Street. This leads you past the Dublin Corporation Fruit and the Vegetable Market to Abbey Street. If you are travelling with children then you must pay a visit to the *Leprechaun Museum* → p. 92 at the corner of Jervis Street. Afterwards you should take the Luas to the final stop at The Point, otherwise you will run out of time. Those without children turn immediately right into Jervis Street, with the Liffey on the left and take the small alley between La Taverna and Bar Italia for a look at *Dublin's Last Supper* → p. 44 by the painter John Byrne and then go along the north bank of the Liffey towards the harbour, past *Custom House* → p. 42 and the *Famine Statues* → p. 48, which honours the victims of the great famine of the mid-1900s. At the end of the street, on the North Wall Quay is Point Village to your left. Climb into one of the gondolas of the 60m/196ft high *Dublin Wheel* → p. 47 and enjoy a fabulous view of Dublin and the Wicklow Mountains.

## 05:30pm MODERN CUISINE AND MUSIC INTO THE NIGHT

Take the Luas back to the Jervis Street station. From here it is a few steps towards the Liffey, then downstream to the Lower Ormond Quay and into the *Winding Stair Bookshop & Restaurant* → p. 58 for a delicious dinner of modern Irish cuisine. Don't stay too long, because now is the time for a stout and some traditional Irish music at the *Cobblestone pub* → p. 73 at Smithfield Square, the largest cobbled square in Dublin, only two stops away on the Luas. If you are still feeling up it after that, go towards the Liffey, left along the north bank and over the Ha'penny Bridge (photo above) to *Temple Bar* → p. 34. There the night continues in pubs and bars until late.

Bus to the starting point,
bus stop: Nassau Street
If you start your day with a full Irish breakfast, you can skip lunch

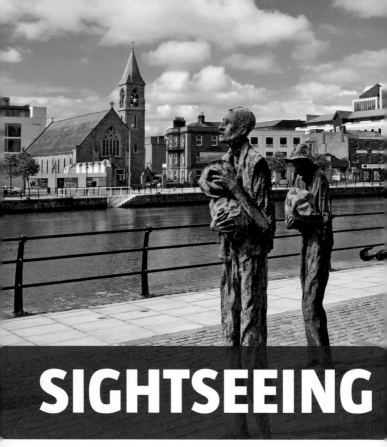

# SIGHTSEEING

**CITY** | **WHERE TO START?**

**(109 D3) (∅ G4) O'Connell Bridge:** a good vantage point from which to get a good overview of the city. North is O'Connell Street, the main thoroughfare, to the east is the old Customs House and the harbor and west is the cast iron Ha'penny Bridge. From here turn right into Fleet Street and you are in the heart of the city's cultural and entertainment district, Temple Bar. *Bus: Burgh Quay/O'Connell Bridge; Luas: Abbey Street*

If you have ever walked your legs off in London or Paris then you will really appreciate Dublin as all the sightseeing attractions are very close to each other in the city centre. The highlights that are not near the city centre can be explored by taking a bus round trip. Dublin offers the tourist so much and yet everything is in a compact and manageable area.

The city's attractions cover all the aspects of its long history. Trinity College with its old library and the magnificent 1200-year-old Book of Kells, two medieval cathedrals (a European rarity) and elegant 18th century squares and buildings, all chronicle the city's development from early

Photo: The Famine Statues at the Custom House Quay

# A city with heart and soul: forget about London, Paris or Rome – Dublin really does offer everything you need

Christian to modern times. It is also full of memorials dedicated to its many literary giants like James Joyce, Oscar Wilde and other famous poets. While the Dubliner's enjoyment of a good tipple is evidenced by the Guinness Brewery and Jameson Whiskey distillery and its many pubs. And their fight for independence is shown in places like Dublin Castle and Kilmainham Gaol.

A small country with a strong cultural history: the Emerald Isle can look back over 9000 years of cultural history and this is a treasure trove for the capital's museums. The city's excellent collections not only include the wealth of the past, but also showcase modern Ireland. Special insights into Irish passions are revealed at the sports museum at Croke Park Stadium, an introduction to Irish literature is best

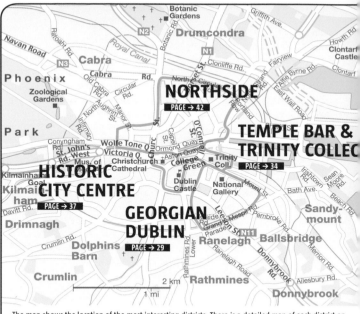

The map shows the location of the most interesting districts. There is a detailed map of each district on which each of the sights described is numbered.

viewed at Dublin Writers Museum while information about the city's history is at the City Hall and the Dublinia. But if you visit only one museum in Dublin, then your choice should be the National Museum of Ireland's Archaeology section filled with the gold treasures that they discovered on the Irish moors and in burial sites. The other world-class institution is the Chester Beatty Library with its remarkable collection of precious manuscripts. Admission to these and all other national museums is free of charge.

Dublin's museums are not only full of local treasures but also contain art treasures from all over Europe and other countries. The National Gallery, and parts of the National Museum, were established during the time of British rule in late 19th century and the early 20th century. Since their independence, the Irish state extended their portfolio and established new museums in some magnificent buildings. Some 18th century barracks house the Decorative Arts and History branch of the National Museum of Ireland while the Museum of Modern Art is in an old Georgian war veterans home with spacious, light-filled rooms in the city district Kilmainham.

The city's most important sightseeing attractions can be reached with three bus stops all along the same route. Take a [INSIDER TIP] round trip with the Dublin Bus and enjoy the live commentary and witty banter of their Dublin bus drivers. They are humorous, irreverent and very well informed *(www.dublinbus.ie / 24 hour ticket 15 euro)*. Another option is the bright green buses from the *Dublin Bus Tours* fleet with a choice of either live commentary from the bus driver or headphone commentary *(www.dublinsightseeing.ie | 24 hour ticket 16 euro, 20 per cent off when booking online)*. But there are also plenty of tours through Dublin on foot or by boat *(p. 103)*. Dublin's most important museums and galleries are either directly in the centre or are within easy reach by public transport. If you buy a 24-hour bus round trip ticket, you can hop off and on directly in front of the following museums (in the order of the trip): National Gallery, Natural History Museum, National Museum – Archaeology, Chester Beatty Library, City Hall, Dublinia, Museum of Modern Art, National Museum – Decorative Arts, Dublin Writers Museum and The Hugh Lane Gallery. There can be no easier route to enjoy a city's art, culture and history!

# GEORGIAN DUBLIN

**The Irish government has made its home in the splendid area around the elegant Merrion Square and St Stephen's Green.** It was in this area in the 18th century that the Georgian architectural era flourished. The resultant streets have long wide boulevards that are flanked by elegant townhouses for the prosperous. The area remains the city's most significant architectural treasure and it is no wonder that parliament, a number of ministries and cultural institutions like the National Museum are based here. The gorgeous gardens on the squares and the banks of the beautiful *Grand Canal* provide lovely relaxation areas.

★ **Merrion Square**
Beautiful examples of Georgian architecture → **p. 31**

★ **National Gallery**
Masterpieces from the late Middle Ages to the 19th century → **p. 32**

★ **National Museum – Archaeology**
Prehistoric gold treasures and precious objects from Ireland's Christian past → **p. 33**

★ **Trinity College**
Where learning blossoms: historic courtyards, the Book of Kells and a remarkable library → **p. 37**

★ **Chester Beatty Library**
Not just for book lovers: exquisite books from different cultures and epochs → **p. 37**

★ **Dublin Castle**
Where British viceroys resided in all their glory → **p. 40**

★ **St Patrick's Cathedral**
1500 years of history in its Gothic architecture and interior → **p. 41**

★ **Guinness Storehouse**
All about the famous stout beer – and some striking city views → **p. 49**

★ **Kilmainham Gaol**
A moving insight into Irish prison history → **p. 50**

★ **Phoenix Park**
A massive public park, the zoo and the head of state's residence → **p. 50**

**MARCO POLO HIGHLIGHTS**

# GEORGIAN DUBLIN

### 1 FITZWILLIAM SQUARE
(115 D3) *(⌘ G6)*

The homes around the square were built between 1791–1825 and some are particularly beautiful examples of the Georgian style. The centre of the square is a large lawn area that is protected by shrubs. In contrast to Merrion Square, this park is not open to the public, but belongs to the owners of the surrounding homes. *Luas/bus: St Stephen's Green*

### 2 GRAND CANAL
(114–115 A3–F1) *(⌘ E6–J5)*

The canal, completed in 1811, was originally an important connection between the city of Dublin and the river Shannon. But today it is not industry that characterises the Grand Canal south of the city centre, instead it is the image of picturesque bridges and locks, trees and elegant townhouses. The part between the Portobello district at Richmond Street and

Georgian style at Fitzwilliam Square

Mount Street Lower makes for an exceptionally beautiful walk along the water. This egg-shaped area, the Grand Canal in the South and its counterpart in the north, the Royal Canal, are boundaries of Dublin and only those born here can call themselves real Dubliners. *DART: Grand Canal Dock, Luas: Charlemont.*

The humble, terraced house *no. 33 Synge Street* near the Grand Canal (114 C3) *(⌘ F6)* is where the playwright and Nobel Prize winner, George Bernard Shaw (1856–1950) spent his first years. The home is furnished in the style of the time and showcases Shaw's life in Dublin. He left his home at 20 as the London literary world held more promise for his career. *May–Sept Mon, Tue, Thu, Fri 10am–1pm, 2pm–5pm, Sat/Sun 2pm–5pm | entrance 7.25 euro | 33 Synge St. | bus: Camden St.*

### 3 INSIDER TIP IVEAGH GARDENS
(114 C3) *(⌘ G6)*

In the middle of Dublin's inner city is an oasis of tranquillity that is often overlooked. Iveagh Gardens might be missing the flowers of the neighbouring St Stephen's Green, but there are many trees, two beautiful fountains carried by angels and spacious lawns perfect for Frisbee players. *Entrances at Clommel St. and Hatch St. Upper | Luas: Harcourt*

### 4 LEINSTER HOUSE
(109 E5) *(⌘ G5)*

The home of the Irish Parliament was built in the classical style in 1745 as a residence for the Dukes of Kildare. This is where both the lower house, called the *Dail*, and the upper house, called the *Seanad*, meet. The Irish like to say that the building was the model for the White House in Washington, which was the work of Irishman James Hoban. *Free admission when not in session | Kildare St. | bus: Nassau St./St Stephen's Green*

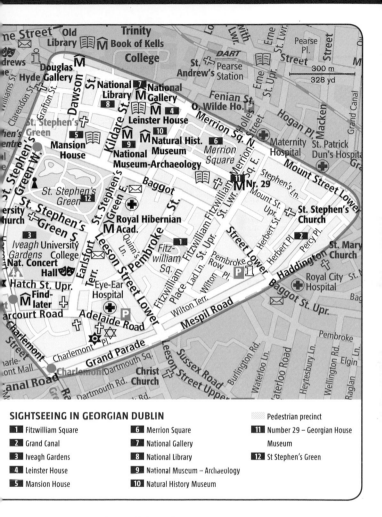

## SIGHTSEEING IN GEORGIAN DUBLIN

**1** Fitzwilliam Square
**2** Grand Canal
**3** Iveagh Gardens
**4** Leinster House
**5** Mansion House

**6** Merrion Square
**7** National Gallery
**8** National Library
**9** National Museum – Archaeology
**10** Natural History Museum

░░░ Pedestrian precinct
**11** Number 29 – Georgian House Museum
**12** St Stephen's Green

**5** **MANSION HOUSE** (109 D5) (*m G5*)
This prestigious residence was built in 1710 by a merchant called Dawson, the local town council liked the building so much that they bought it in 1715 and since then it has been used as the mayor's residence. The round hall, where in 1919 the new Irish Parliament had their first meeting, was built specifically to ac-

commodate King George IV on his visit.
*Dawson St. | no viewing | Luas/bus: St Stephen's Green*

**6** **MERRION SQUARE** ★ ●
(109 F5–6) (*m G–H5*)
Since the 1770s Merrion Square has been one of the finest addresses in Dublin. It is well known for its typically Georgian

National Gallery: let the masterpieces take you on a tour through European art history

architecture, its colourful doors and the beautiful park in the middle of the square. There is also a collection of historical street lamps and an old air raid bunker in the south-east corner. Daniel O'Connell (no. 58), William Butler Yeats (no. 84) and Oscar Wilde's family (no. 2 at the north-east corner, now the *American College* and infrequently open to the public) all lived in Merrion Square. For many years Wilde's books were banned in Ireland but now there is an unusual statue of him across from his former home. Oscar Wilde himself would have loved the colourful statue, because it really does capture his persona very well. The dandy and man of letters is sprawled with provocative ease on a boulder looking towards his family home. *Bus: Merrion Square*

### ◼ NATIONAL GALLERY ★
(109 E5) (*ⅢG5*)

The world-class art collection includes masterpieces from all over Europe from the 14th to the 20th century. The Italian section is one of the most impressive with works by Fra Angelico, Titian and Michelangelo Caravaggio, whose ● 'The Taking of Christ' is probably the most significant painting in the entire collection. Also on display are works by Spanish painters like Diego Velazquez, Francisco de Goya and Pablo Picasso, French masters like Nicolas Poussin and the Impressionists as well as German and Dutch works like those by Emil Nolde and Peter Paul Ruben which all hang in its magnificent 19th century halls. British and Irish artists are given priority, such as portrait painters Thomas Gainsborough and Joshua Reynolds as well as the most significant Irish artist of the 20th century, Jack Butler Yeats. The *National Portrait Collection* shows portraits of leading personalities from Irish society. In the new wing of the National Gallery is the popular *Museum café. Mon–Sat 9.30am–5.30pm (Thu until 8.30pm), Sun midday–5.30pm | free admission |*

*Merrion Square West and Clare St. | www. nationalgallery.ie | bus: Merrion Square*

### 8 INSIDER TIP NATIONAL LIBRARY
(109 E5) (ω G5)

Directly north of Leinster House is the National Library, a magnificent building that dates back to the 19th century. The ornate entrance hall staircase leads up to the large reading room with a glass roof, a colourful frieze and ceiling mouldings. The original furnishings include shelves with wood carvings and tables with green reading lamps. *Mon–Sat 9.30am–5.30pm (Thu until 8.30pm), Sun midday–5.30pm | free admission | Merrion Square West and Clare St. | www.nationalgallery.ie | bus: Merrion Square*

### 9 NATIONAL MUSEUM – ARCHAEOLOGY ★ ●
(109 E5) (ω G5)

If you wanted to fill an ark with all the objects that document Ireland's rich his-

tory, then you would use all the exhibits in this museum. Here you can see well-preserved Bronze Age weapons and horns (used as instruments) and some really remarkable gold treasures: wonderfully crafted collars, bangles, gold earrings and gold filaments.

One of the rarities from early Christian times is the 1200 year-old *Ardagh* Chalice and the *Tara Brooch*, crafted around the year 700 and decorated with Celtic patterns. An ancient bog body, a dugout canoe dating from about 2500 BC, Viking finds and medieval artefacts are just some of its many highlights. The museum also houses a good Egyptology collection. *Tue–Sat 10am–5pm, Sun 2pm–5pm | free admission | Kildare St. | www.museum.ie | bus: Merrion Square, St Stephen's Green*

### 10 NATURAL HISTORY MUSEUM
(109 E5) (ω G5)

Irreverent Dubliners call it the 'Dead Zoo'. At the entrance you are greeted by the skeletons of some of the Irish elks that lived here 10,000 years ago. The *Irish Room* on the ground floor is dedicated to indigenous animals, while the top floor has animals from around the world. Even after extensive renovations the museum has kept its Victorian charm – it has remained a kind of museum within a museum. *Tue–Sat 10am–5pm, Sun 2pm–5pm | free admission | Merrion St. | www.museum.ie | bus: Merrion Square West*

### 11 NUMBER 29 – GEORGIAN HOUSE MUSEUM (109 F6) (ω H5)

The five floors of this restored and furnished city home showcase the lifestyle of well off Dubliners in the 1800s. The tour guide takes you through life in the kitchen and the housekeeper's room in the basement, the expensively furnished dining and living rooms and the bedrooms and children's rooms on the first floor.

*Only with a guide Tue–Sat 10am–5pm, Sun midday–5pm | 6 euro | 29 Fitzwilliam St. Lower | bus: Merrion Square*

### 🔟 ST STEPHEN'S GREEN
(109 D6) *(ᗰ G5–6)*

A lot remains of the original 18th century buildings on the eastern side of the square. The other sides show – in varying degrees – the planning errors since the 1960s, but are still worth seeing. The imposing *Royal College of Surgeons* on the west side still shows traces of the battles fought during the rebellion of 1916. James Joyce studied in the Catholic University *Newman House* on the south side *(June–Aug Tue–Fri 2pm–5pm, tours 2pm, 3pm, 4pm | 5 euro)*. Right next door is the INSIDER TIP *University Church*, a small jewel in the neo-Byzantine style of the 19th century. One of the most beautiful of the attractions is the park in the middle, which was private property in the 1850s.

Since the 1880s it has been open to the public, thanks to the generosity of Lord Ardilaun from the Guinness family. *Luas/bus: St. Stephen's Green*

# TEMPLE BAR & TRINITY COLLEGE

**Temple Bar is both a cultural and an entertainment district. The small alleyways and houses of the old merchant district were supposed to be demolished in the 1980s to make way for a new bus terminal.**

But instead, the rundown and dilapidated area became a magnet for the creative set, the potential of the area on the Liffey was acknowledged and a renovation that preserved the Temple Bar's character was

St Stephen's Green: a city park that is open to the public thanks to a Guinness patron

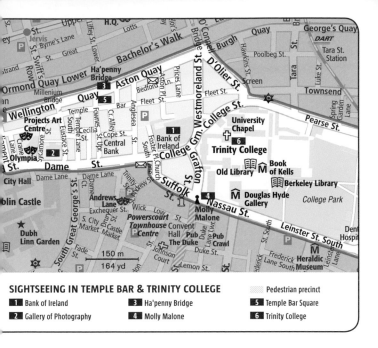

## SIGHTSEEING IN TEMPLE BAR & TRINITY COLLEGE

| | | | |
|---|---|---|---|
| **1** Bank of Ireland | **3** Ha'penny Bridge | **5** Temple Bar Square | |
| **2** Gallery of Photography | **4** Molly Malone | **6** Trinity College | |

▨ Pedestrian precinct

begun. Nowadays during the day there is a vibrant and relaxed atmosphere in the arty and trendy cafés, shops, designer boutiques and music stores while in the evenings the city district becomes a cultural zone for film and music fans, and turns into a loud and popular party location. Right next to the buzzing Temple Bar are two venerable institutions: the *Bank of Ireland* in the old Parliament building and the old University *Trinity College*, one of Dublin's major attractions.

### **1** BANK OF IRELAND
### (109 D4) (*ℳ G5*)

The bank building with its imposing façade was used in the 18th century as the Irish Parliament. Everyone is welcome to stroll in to admire the wonderful main hall or to warm themselves at the fireplace in the hallways. Tour guides with a lot of knowledge about Irish history lead tours through the House of Lords with its crystal chandeliers, tapestries and Irish oak panelled walls. *Main hall Mon–Fri 10am–4pm, free tour only Tue 10.30am, 11.30am, 1.45pm | College Green | bus: Nassau St.*

### **2** GALLERY OF PHOTOGRAPHY
### (108 C4) (*ℳ F5*)

This gallery in the middle of the Temple Bar is Ireland's leading establishment for contemporary photography and is the place where top Irish photographers exhibit their most recent works. There is also a good photo book shop attached to the gallery. On the opposite side of the square is the *Photographic Archive*, which also has temporary exhibitions free of charge. *Tue–Sat 11am–6pm, Sun 1pm–6pm | Meeting House Square | galleryofphotography.ie | bus: Temple Bar*

At Temple Bar Square culture is always within easy reach, not only at the book market

### ▨ HA'PENNY BRIDGE

(108 C3) (*G5*)

The bridge was built in 1816 as Wellington Bridge but the toll (which was in place until 1919) gave it its present day name of Halfpenny Bridge. The beautiful cast iron bridge connects the pubs and clubs north of the Liffey with the stone *Merchants Arch*, which leads into the Temple Bar district. *Bus: Aston Quay*

### ▨ MOLLY MALONE

(109 D4) (*G5*)

Every Irishman knows the ballad about the buxom beauty: 'In Dublin's fair city, where girls are so pretty, I first set my eyes on sweet Molly Malone ...'. During the day she sold fish, and at night she sold herself. According to legend, Molly was a fishmonger's daughter from Fishamble Street in Temple Bar, who died in 1699. But there is no proof that she actually lived. *On the west side of Grafton St. near the entrance to Trinity College | bus: Nassau St.*

### ▨ TEMPLE BAR SQUARE

(108 C4) (*G5*)

This small square is the heart of the Temple Bar district, surrounded as it is with small inviting pubs and restaurants. In the evening there is live music in many of the establishments while the young musicians, who are unable to gig in the pubs, try their luck busking on the pavements. On weekends most Dubliners prefer to find their entertainment elsewhere, but during the day and in the week Temple Bar Square and the adjacent alleys are civilized enough. Culture is always at ones fingertips here: the *Irish Film Institute* with its art-house cinema is only two minutes away in Eustace Street. To the west on East Essex Street is the *Project Arts Centre*, with two stages and a gallery, while *Temple Bar Music Centre*, with studios and concert venue, is just around the corner in Curved Street. On weekends a small book market is held on the square. More info: *www.visit-templebar.com | bus: Aston Quay, Dame St.*

### 6 TRINITY COLLEGE ★
(109 D4) *(ⵑ G5)*

Everyone is allowed to stroll freely through the old courtyards and admire the grey classical façades of the university that was founded in 1592. Some of its famous alumni are writers such as Jonathan Swift, Dracula creator Bram Stoker, Oscar Wilde and Samuel Beckett.

The college also has two special highlights (for a small fee): the beautiful Book of Kells and the 18th century library. The Book of Kells is a 680-page exquisitely illustrated handwritten manuscript of the four Gospels. It is believed to have originated around the year 800 on the Scottish island of Iona and then given to the monastery of Kells (in county Meath) to safeguard it against Viking raids. The attractive exhibition explains many aspects of the manuscript from the manufacture of the colour pigments and the calf leather to the symbolism used as well as the way of life in the monasteries. A flight of stairs leads up to the spectacular, barrel vaulted *Long Room*, where about 200,000 manuscripts are kept. Particularly impressive are the wood carvings on the high bookshelves, the line of busts of Irish writers and scientists and the oldest Irish harp which dates back to the late Middle Ages. *Mon–Sat 9.30am–5pm, Sun May–Sept 9.30am–4.30pm, Oct–April midday–4.30pm | 9 euro for Book of Kells and Long Room | College St. | www.tcd.ie | bus: Nassau St.*

# HISTORIC CITY CENTRE

**In the Middle Ages the trading city of Dublin extended a mile south from the river Liffey and the city's ancient main roads still exists today as Dame Street, Lord Edward Street and High Street.**
To the left and right of them is evidence of the city's chequered past like its two medieval cathedrals and Dublin Castle, where the British tried to rule Ireland for 750 years. Today the area has a mixed character, it is partly a shopping and tourist district, but also has commercial office buildings, apartments and homes.

### 1 CHESTER BEATTY LIBRARY ★
(108 B5) *(ⵑ F5)*

This museum was a gift to the Irish nation from the American mining millionaire Sir Alfred Chester Beatty (1875–1968) and

## RELAX & ENJOY

Those in need of relaxation can opt for the luxurious wellness spa at the edge of the Wicklow Mountains, an hour's drive south of Dublin: ● *Wells Spa* **(0)** *(ⵑ 0)* at the Brook Lodge Hotel. Finnish baths, aromatherapy baths and hammam massages ensure total relaxation. The pool water is from the hotel's own wells *(Macreddin Village | County Wicklow | tel. 0402 3 64 44 | www.brooklodge.com).* In the city you can be pampered with the massage and beauty services at ● *Therapie* **(109 D5)** *(ⵑ G5) (9 Molesworth Street | tel. 01 4 72 12 22 | www.therapie.ie)* or at the *Merrion Hotel* **(109 E6)** *(ⵑ G5) (Upper Merrion Street | tel.01 6 03 06 00 | www.merrionhotelcom).* At Temple Bar you can relax at ● *Mai Thai Massage* **(108 C4)** *(ⵑ F5)* with their traditional Thai practices *(6 Crow Street | tel. 08 62 50 86 43 | www.maithaimassage.ie).*

houses unique objects, manuscripts and exhibits from a number of different cultures. Some of the highlights are papyrus scrolls with the gospels of Mark and Luke from the year 200, precious Koran exhibits from Turkey, Iran and India, wonderful Buddhist and Far Eastern book art. And it also includes rare jade writings from the Chinese imperial court, medieval manuscripts and early European print specimens.

The permanent exhibition consists of two main parts: one for the sacred and one for the artistic tradition of manuscript illustrations. The museum regularly presents different temporary exhibitions with treasures from its archives. *Tue–Fri 10am–5pm, Sat 11am–5pm, Sun 1pm–5pm, May–Sept also Mon 10am–5pm |* *free admission | on the grounds of Dublin Castle | entrance at Dame St. or Ship St. | www.cbl.ie*

## ■2 CHRIST CHURCH CATHEDRAL
(108 B4) (*ᗰ F5*)

In the Middle Ages Dublin was the only city in Europe with two cathedrals. St Patrick's Cathedral was probably built to replace the older Christ Church Cathedral as the bishop's seat. This failed and both churches kept their status as a cathedral. The Christ Church Cathedral, which is more than 800 years old – and Anglican like St Patrick's – underwent extensive restoration in the 19th century and was remodelled in the early Gothic style. Only parts of the transept shows Romanesque elements from the time around 1171, when the Norman Richard de Clare (known as Strongbow) had the old wooden building replaced with a new stone one. Strongbow's tomb in the south nave was once the place where oaths or agreements were concluded amongst merchants.

The cathedral has two INSIDER TIP curiosities: the first is a display case with the mummified remains of a cat and a rat, which were found in an organ pipe. The second is in the south-east Peace Chapel where there is a heart-shaped relic made out of iron, which houses Archbishop Laurence O'Toole's heart. He died in 1180 and was sanctified in 1230. In the crypt you can also view church treasures, gravestones as well as a film about the history of its construction. *Daily 9.45am–5pm, June–Aug 9am–6pm, no viewing during mass | 6 euro | Christchurch Place | www.cccdub.ie | bus: Lord Edward St.*

The art of books at the Chester Beatty Library

## ■3 CITY HALL
(108 B4) (*ᗰ F5*)

Dublin's merchants had the classical dome building erected as a stock exchange in 1779 but in 1851 it became the City Hall.

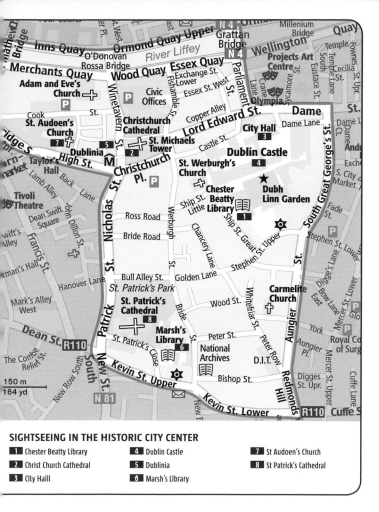

## SIGHTSEEING IN THE HISTORIC CITY CENTER

1 Chester Beatty Library
2 Christ Church Cathedral
3 City Halll
4 Dublin Castle
5 Dublinia
6 Marsh's Library
7 St Audoen's Church
8 St Patrick's Cathedral

The rotunda has an impressive dome and is also where you can see a 6m/19ft high statue of Daniel O'Connell, who became the city's first Catholic mayor (since the Reformation) in 1841. The vaulted cellar under the City Hall houses an exhibition that traces Dublin's history from its beginnings to today. The displays and audiovisual presentations convey a detailed picture of the city in the times of the Vikings and Normans, during the Middle Ages and in its heyday in the 18th century. It also includes references to the city's urban development problems in the 19th and 20th centuries. *Mon–Sat 10am–5.15pm | Dame St./cnr Parliament St. | entrance 4 euro | www.dublincity.ie | bus: Dame St.*

# HISTORIC CITY CENTRE

## 4 DUBLIN CASTLE ⭐
(108 B4) (*ⓜ F5*)

All that remains from the original early 13th century building is one mighty tower which survived the explosion of the gunpowder storage room in the 17th century. section where you see part of the city wall that dates from the Viking times and a tower dating to 1234. *Mon–Fri 10am–4.45pm, Sat–Sun 2pm–4.45pm | 4.50 euro | Dame St. | www.dublincastle.ie | bus: Dame St.*

The viceroys have left, but their glory remains: the Drawing Room at the Dublin Castle

The old castle was replaced with a magnificent palace for the Crown. In 1922 the castle was handed over to the independent Irish state and used for official and ceremonial events. Carpets from Donegal and chandeliers made from Waterford crystal all represent the new independent Ireland, but the portraits of the British viceroys also still hang here. During the one-hour tour visitors can view the splendid 18th and 19th century halls, such as the glittering ballroom, the throne room and the banquet hall with its gilded furniture. The tour finishes off with an underground

## 5 DUBLINIA
(108 A4) (*ⓜ F5*)

Here you can immerse yourself in the world of the Vikings, the Normans and the medieval era. The exhibition is in a beautiful neo-Gothic building that once served as the cathedral's Synod Hall and consists mainly of recreated scenes and audio-visual displays. But the visit is still worth it, especially for the vivid representation of the Vikings' lives with their ships, tools and weapons. *April–Sept daily 10am–5pm, Oct–March Mon–Fri 11am–4pm, Sat–Sun 10am–4pm | entrance fee*

*6.95 euro | St Michaels Hill, Christ Church Cathedral | www.dublinia.ie | bus: Lord Edward St.*

### 6 INSIDERTIP MARSH'S LIBRARY
(108 B6) *(ひ F5)*

Near St Patrick's Cathedral is the wonderful Marsh's Library that dates back to 1701. It is Ireland's oldest public library. There are tens of thousands of books and manuscripts on magnificent neoclassical shelves that are decorated with the mitre and flower, symbols of its founder Archbishop Narcissus March. *Mon, Wed–Fri 10am–1pm, 2pm–5pm, Sat 10.30am–1pm | 2.50 euro | St Patrick's Close | www.marsh library.ie | bus: 49, 49A, 49B, 50, 54A, 56A, 65, 65B, 77, 77A from Eden Quay*

### 7 ST AUDOEN'S CHURCH
(108 A4) *(ひ F5)*

Two rather different churches but both have the Norman, Saint Ouen as their patron saints. The neoclassical façade on the right belongs to the Catholic Church from the 19th century. The unimposing Anglican Church on the left's foundation was laid in 1190. The adjacent visitor centre has all the information about its colourful history. A popular highlight of the tour is the *Lucky Stone*, a gravestone from the 7th century that is purported to bring luck and which generations of believers have kissed and touched. *Visitor Centre May–Oct daily 9.30am–5.30pm | High St. | bus: Lord Edward St.*

### 8 ST PATRICK'S CATHEDRAL ★
(108 B6) *(ひ F5)*

The Anglican St Patrick's Cathedral displays the history of the Anglo-Irish families that ruled Ireland for centuries. Its interior is full of the tombs of dignitaries and memorials commemorating the British Empire's wars in China and Burma. The cathedral was built in the early 13th century in the Gothic style in place of the older buildings, which possibly go back to the wooden church of St Patrick. The Boyle family's four-storey tomb is impressive as is the much-visited memorial for writer Jonathan Swift, who was also once a dean at the cathedral. The wooden door in the north transept has an unusual history attached to it: during a feud between the Earls of Ormond and Kildare in 1492, Ormond locked himself in the cathedral's chapter house. Kildare wanted to end the conflict so he knocked a hole into the door and put his hand through as a peace offering.

St Patrick's Park next to the cathedral is the place – according to tradition – where Patrick converted and baptised 450 people to Christianity and it is a pleasant place for a break. Niches in the wall on the east side of the park are dedicated to important Irish writers. *Mon–Sat 9am–6pm, Sun 9am–11am, 12.45pm–3pm, 4.15pm–6pm |*

## LOW BUDGET

▶ These outstanding Dublin facilities all offer free admission: the *National Museum – Archaeology,* the *National Museum – Decorative Arts and History*, the *National Gallery*, the *Natural History Museum*, the *Chester Beatty Library*, the *Irish Museum of Modern Art* and the *Hugh Lane Gallery*.

▶ *Dublin Bus* offers a variety of reasonably priced passes, for example the 3 day *Rambler Ticket* for all lines incl. the airport bus 747 and 748 *(13.30 euro)* or the 3 day Freedom Ticket *(26 euro)* which includes a round trip with commentary. Available at the airport and 59 Upper O'Connell Street.

*entrance fee 5.50 euro | St Patrick's Close | www.stpatrickscathedral.ie | bus: 49, 49A, 49B, 50, 54A, 56A, 65, 65B, 77, 77A from Eden Quay*

Anglican stronghold: St Patrick's

# NORTHSIDE

**The area north of the Liffey riverbank combines various historical aspects of the Irish capital so this is where you will find medieval Dublin (St Michan's Church), Georgian Dublin (the Custom House) as well as 18th century stately homes.**

The chic hotels and bars in the immediate vicinity of the river are reminders of Dublin's financial boom years, whilst a few streets away the buildings are still waiting to be restored to their former glory and the department stores attract working class customers with their cheap prices. For the tourist this district offers a vibrant and colourful mix of interesting museums, the wide boulevard of *O'Connell Street* and some good theatres.

### ■1 CUSTOM HOUSE
### (109 E2) (*□ G4*)

The Custom House, completed in 1791 by Irish architect James Gandon, is probably the most magnificent example of Georgian Dublin's heyday. Its 100m/328ft wide façade fronts on to the Liffey and includes a high domed tower, a series of beautiful sculptures with 14 allegorical heads which symbolise Ireland's rivers, the statues *Hibernia* (Ireland) and *Britannia* in the pediment as well as cattle heads which represent the country's once flourishing beef trade. The best view of the entire building is from the *Talbot Memorial Bridge* east of the railway bridge. *Not open to the public at the moment | Custom House Quay | DART: Connolly/ Tara Street.*

### ■2 DUBLIN WRITERS MUSEUM
### (112 C5) (*□ F4*)

The exhibition, in two Georgian houses, is dedicated to what the Irish are most

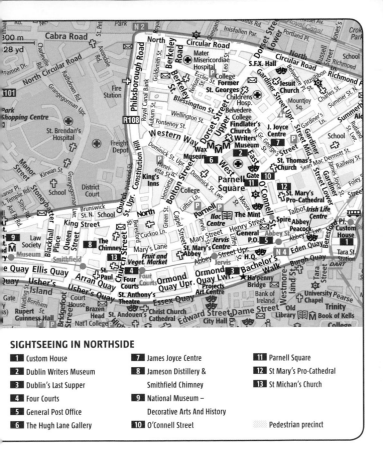

## SIGHTSEEING IN NORTHSIDE

**1** Custom House

**2** Dublin Writers Museum

**3** Dublin's Last Supper

**4** Four Courts

**5** General Post Office

**6** The Hugh Lane Gallery

**7** James Joyce Centre

**8** Jameson Distillery & Smithfield Chimney

**9** National Museum – Decorative Arts And History

**10** O'Connell Street

**11** Parnell Square

**12** St Mary's Pro-Cathedral

**13** St Michan's Church

///// Pedestrian precinct

proud of: their great literary tradition. Here you can learn about the life and works of Nobel Prize winner William Butler Yeats, George Bernard Shaw and Samuel Beckett. Also honoured are Oscar Wilde, James Joyce and playwrights like Richard Brinsley Sheridan and Brendan Behan. The history of Irish literature is displayed with curiosities such as a letter from George Bernard Shaw in which he refuses to give an autograph, but then signs the letter himself. The museum also boasts a nice café with garden terrace and a well-stocked bookstore. If you would like to experience a beautiful Georgian interior visit the **INSIDER TIP** café and bookstore without having to pay a museum admission fee. The *Irish Writers Centre* next door at no. 19 holds readings and seminars. *Mon–Sat 10am–5pm (June–Aug until 6pm), Sun 11am–5pm | entrance 7.50 euro, combined ticket 11.50 euro for the Dublin Writers Museum and the Shaw Birthplace or the James Joyce Museum | 18 Parnell Square | www.writersmuseum.com | bus: Parnell Square*

### 3 DUBLIN'S LAST SUPPER
(108 C3) *(∅ F5)*

*Dublin's Last Supper*, the Irish version of Leonardo da Vinci's masterpiece, represents the changes within Irish society and its new cultural diversity. The large artwork is in a courtyard in the *Italian Quarter* on the Liffey and was created by the Northern Irish artist John Byrne. It consists of 13 photographs of locals, whom Byrne met on the streets of Dublin. *Blooms Lane, Lower Ormond Quay | Luas: Jervis*

troops. Today the Four Courts have been restored and are in use as the courthouse. *Open to the public but no tours | Inns Quay | Luas: Four Courts*

### 5 GENERAL POST OFFICE (GPO)
(109 D2) *(∅ G4)*

The main post office was used as the headquarters of the rebels during the 1916 Easter Rising and has since become a national shrine. After its destruction in 1916, the neoclassical building was re-

The Four Courts courthouse, built in 1802, with its characteristic dome

### 4 FOUR COURTS
(108 A3) *(∅ F5)*

The court house was completed in 1802 and the building, with its high dome, is a striking landmark on the Liffey's north bank. It was badly damaged in the 1921 civil war when opponents of the treaty with Great Britain took refuge in the building until they were forced out by the artillery shelling of the new government's

stored by the Irish government. Its counters, post boxes and tables – made from marble, dark wood and shiny brass – make it worth a visit. On the façade outside you can still see bullet holes. In case you need stamps, and there is a long queue at the post office, it is worth going into the INSIDER TIP *Philatelic Office* left of the main entrance. It is usually empty and you can get beautiful commemorative stamps here. *O'Connell St. open during business hours | bus: O'Connell St.*

## 6 THE HUGH LANE GALLERY
(108 C1) (*F4*)

Sir Hugh Lane's art collection forms the basis of the city's art museum and covers the full spectrum of works from Impressionists like Monet, Manet and Degas through to contemporary artists. The aristocratic 18th century residence, Charlemont House, is the perfect setting for it. The gallery exhibits contemporary Irish and international artists and acquired the complete London studio (with its creative chaos) of the Dublin-born Francis Bacon (1909–92) and recreated it at the museum. *Tue–Thu 10am–6pm, Fri–Sat 10am–5pm, Sun 11am–5pm | free admission to the permanent exhibition, Francis Bacon Studio 7 euro | Parnell Square North | www.hugh lane.ie | bus: Parnell Square*

## 7 JAMES JOYCE CENTRE
(112 C5) (*G4*)

This exhibition, in a Georgian townhouse near the Dublin Writers Museum, highlights the life and works of James Joyce. Temporary exhibitions, lectures, seminars and guided walks are also on offer here. *Tue–Sat 10am–5pm | entrance 5 euro | 35 North Great George's St. | bus: O'Connell St.*

## 8 JAMESON DISTILLERY AND SMITHFIELD CHIMNEY
(114 B1) (*F4*)

The visitors centre, in a disused distillery, offers some good insights into the fine art of whiskey distilling. The tour, which includes sampling, doesn't hold back on promoting the product, but is nonetheless entertaining and informative. The distillery's 60m/196ft high chimney has a lift that goes up to a glass ⚡ observation deck. From here the view extends from over the rehabilitated Smithfield

area (where new apartments have been cleverly integrated into the old buildings around the Jameson Whiskey Distillery) to the Liffey and over the city centre. *Distillery daily 9.30am–6pm | admission fee 12.50 euro | Chimney Mon–Sat 10am–5.30pm, Sun 11am–5.30pm | entrance 5 euro | Smithfield Village | Luas: Smithfield*

## 9 NATIONAL MUSEUM – DECORATIVE ARTS AND HISTORY
(114 A1) (*E4*)

The splendidly restored 18th and 19th century *Collins Barracks* served as barracks for almost 300 years. Today they house a significant art collection, which covers all the areas of the applied arts. The extended group of buildings, which are situated around a central courtyard, has exhibits of weapons, furniture, ceramics, fashion, silver and glass from many different centuries. Irish folk art is also well represented, as well as Chinese porcelain and European arts and crafts. Temporary exhibitions highlight different themes from Irish history. The INSIDER TIP ► *Curator's Room* is a great source of inspiration for any visitor. Here the museum's curators show and explain their favourite pieces. *Tue–Sat 10am–5pm, Sun 2pm–5pm | free admission | Benburb St. | www.museum.ie | Luas: Museum, bus 90 from Aston Quay, 25, 66 and 67 from Wellington Quay*

## 10 O'CONNELL STREET
(109 D1–3) (*G4*)

Dublin's impressive thoroughfare honours the gifted orator who fought for the equal rights of Catholics in the first half of the 19th century – Daniel O'Connell (1775–1847). His memory is enthroned by an impressive memorial on the south side of the street. After extensive renovations the street is once more deserving of its reputation as a grand and imposing boulevard. One of the most remarkable monuments is on

We will never know what James Joyce would have made of the Millennium Spire

the median strip, the *Monument of Light* (also called the *Millennium Spire*) a 120m/392ft high, impressive shining steel needle that sparkles over Dublin's rooftops at night. Admiral Nelson looked down on this spot from a pillar until 1966, but on the 50th anniversary of the 1916 Easter rising, the IRA blew up this symbol of British rule.

A bit further north you will come across the statue of *Father Matthew* holding up his right hand in warning. In the middle of the 19th century the Carmelite monk preached to the masses urging them to abstain from alcohol. He only achieved moderate success: today of all the Europeans, only the Finns drink more alcohol than the Irish. Today Dublin's south side might be more stylish than O'Connell Street, but the department store *Clery's* and the *Gresham Hotel* are reminders of its elegant past.

## ▇▇ PARNELL SQUARE
**(108 C1) (*ⁿ F−G4*)**

Charles Steward Parnell (1849–91) fought for the fair treatment of Ireland's rural poor and for an independent Irish parliament. His monument at the north end of O'Connell Street marks the south-east corner of Parnell Square. The *Rotunda Hospital,* a maternity hospital, was built in 1752 and occupies the southern centre of the square. In the rotunda next door, today a concert hall, high society once met to raise funds to cover the cost of nursing care. The northern half of the square is dedicated to the *Garden of Remembrance*, a memorial for all who died in the fight for Ireland's independence. With flower beds and benches around a cross-shaped pond, the garden offers INSIDER TIP the best place near O'Connell Street to enjoy a break. *Bus: Parnell Square*

## 12 ST MARY'S PRO-CATHEDRAL ●
### (109 D2) (*ΜΏ G4*)

The Roman Catholic cathedral is hidden away down a side street. Only after the emancipation of the Catholics in 1829 were their churches allowed to be part of the cityscape. St Mary's was built in 1816 in the Greek style with modest proportions. INSIDER TIP During Sunday mass, the excellent Palestrina Choir performs here *(11 am). Marlborough St. bus: O'Connell St.*

## 13 ST MICHAN'S CHURCH
### (108 A3) (*ΜΏ F4*)

The main attraction of this church, which was built in 1685, is not its beautiful 19th century interior, but the vaults underneath. The extremely dry air of the church's crypts have mummified the corpses buried there and prevented their decay. One of the corpses in the macabre display apparently belongs to a crusader who died 650 years ago but it is not entirely certain if the tomb really does date back to the Middle Ages. *Tours Mon–Fri 5pm March–Oct 10am–12.45pm and 2pm–4.30pm, Nov–16 March 12.30pm –3.30pm, Sat all year round 10am–12.45pm | 4 euro | Church St. | Luas: Four Courts*

# IN OTHER DISTRICTS

## DOCKLANDS (109 F2) (*ΜΏ G–J4*)

When the docks, ports and storage warehouses at the Liffey near the city centre became too small for modern merchant ships, the old harbour district slowly declined. But as in so many other European cities, the Dubliners also soon discovered the charms of living and working directly on the waterfront and an urban renewal saw modern steel and glass palaces built along the Liffey banks. And the once-neglected Docklands is now considered a landmark development that serves as a reminder of Ireland's economic boom time when it was one of Europe's wealthiest countries. Some of the main attractions in this area are architect Daniel Libeskind's *Grand Canal Theatre*, the *Convention Centre* with its glass atrium, the *Samuel Beckett Bridge* as well as *Point Village*. It is also where you will find Dublin's latest attraction, the ⚡ *Big Wheel*, a 60m/196ft high Ferris wheel where you can sway in a gondola high above the Irish capital and

# KEEP FIT!

With an area of 1750 acres, Phoenix Park is double the size of New York's Central Park, giving you plenty of space to jog! The ambitious can go full circle (11km/7mi) but there shorter routes throughout the park or you can also take a bicycle ride *(Phoenix Park Bike Hire | Chesterfield Ave | tel. 08 62 65 62 58)*. If you would rather smell the sea air, drive to the coast where Malahide Beach *(117 F4) (ΜΏ 0)*

has great jogging tracks. Swimmers who dare to enter the chilly waters of the Irish Sea best do so at *Forty Foot* in Sandycove *(117 F5) (ΜΏ 0)* or at the *Markievicz Leisure Centre* *(109 E3) (ΜΏ G5)* in the middle of the city centre, where you can swim in the swimming pool *(Mon–Fri 7am–10pm, Sat 9am–6pm, Sun 10am–4pm | Townsend St. near Trinity College | DART: Tara Street).*

get a wonderful view of the distant mountains of Wicklow *(Mon–Sat 10am–9pm, Sun 10am–7pm | admission fee 9 euro, children (4–16 years) 6.50 euro, family ticket 23 euro | Luas: The Point).*

On the north side of the Liffey, east of the Custom House, are the *Famine Statues*, a modern memorial to the lives lost in the terrible famine of the 1840s. They are a series of tragically thin figures and well worth seeing. Over a million Irish died during that time and many more emigrated. The tall ship *Jeanie Johnston*, a reproduction of the 1847 'famine ship', is anchored at the Sean O'Casey Bridge. *DART/Luas: Connolly Station*

## THE LIBERTIES
(114 A–B2) *(₥ E–F5)*

During the Middle Ages the landowners of this area, west of the city wall, enjoyed special rights and privileges called 'liberties'. Today there are no such privileges and the area around Thomas Street and Meath Street is much the same as any ordinary suburb. But in Francis Street there are still a few antique shops that cater to connoisseurs and the wealthy. The antithesis of the chic shopping area – around Grafton Street in the centre – is the *Liberty Market (Meath Street, Thu–Sat)*, where you can find inexpensive groceries and clothing alongside household items and communion dresses. Behind St Catherine's Church is a small grotto with a statue of Mary, testament to Ireland's strong Catholic character. **INSIDER TIP** The St Augustine Church on Thomas Street is a marvel of neo-Gothic architecture built in 1862–1895. The interior is opulent and colourful: stained glass windows from a Munich workshop and from Irish artists, a white Carrara marble altar, colourfully painted holy statues and mosaics together with countless wax and electrical candles all turn the church into a sparkling treasure. *Bus: 121, 123 from O'Connell St.*

Futuristic vision from the days of prosperity: Samuel Beckett Bridge and the Congress Centre

# MORE SITES

### GAA MUSEUM (113 D4) *(𝄐 G3)*

Sport is more than just a hobby for the Irish and the exhibition, at the home of the GAA (Gaelic Athletic Association) in the Croke Park Stadium, doesn't simply offer trophy collections but nurtures Irish sports like *hurling* and *Gaelic football* which form an integral part of the Irish national identity. The interactive museum explains the political and cultural aspects of the sport. *Mon–Sat 9.30am–5pm, Sun midday–5pm | admission fee 6 euro | Croke Park | St Joseph's Avenue | www.gaa.ie | bus: 3, 11, 16, 123 from O'Connell St.*

### GLASNEVIN CEMETERY (112 A2) *(𝄐 E2)*

The mission statement of this cemetery, which hangs at the entrance, is to 'Preserve the Past for Future Generations'. The cemetery – officially known as *Prospect*

*Cemetery* – is Dublin's answer to the Père Lachaise in Paris. More than 1.2 million people are buried here: the rich and the powerful, the famous and the infamous, the poor and the unknown. Many notable figures from the Irish struggle for independence are laid to rest here, specifically Daniel O'Connell, whose crypt is in a particularly impressive round tower near the main entrance. The beautifully crafted reliefs on the gravestones are worth the visit, many carry the Celtic cross with the sun symbol or the typically Irish decorative patterns entwined with mythical creatures. The cemetery is as secure as a fort with a 4m/13ft high wall with watchtowers which were used as protection against grave robbers. Fresh corpses were worth a lot of money at the beginning of the 19th century when physicians needed a constant supply for their anatomical examinations. After the round trip a INSIDER TIP▶ break in the cosy Kavanagh's pub at Prospect Square is highly recommended. *Daily 9am–4.30pm, guided tours in winter daily 2.30pm, in the summer 2–3 times a day | 8 euro | Finglas Road | bus: 40, 40A, 40B, 40C from Parnell St.*

The *Museum*, below the souvenir shop and café, has won numerous awards the most recent being the best International Museum 2011 *(Mon–Fri 10am–5pm, Sat–Sun 11am–5pm | entrance 6 euro, combined ticket cemetery tour and museum 9.60 euro | www.glasnevinmuseum.ie).*

### GUINNESS STOREHOUSE ★ (114 A2) *(𝄐 E5)*

Housed in a spectacularly converted 19th century factory warehouse, this is where the *Guinness Company* reveals all the steps in the brewing process and includes traditional processes and excellent recreations. An absolute highlight is the ☘ *Gravity Bar,* a glass rotunda on the roof, where every visitor receives a *pint of*

*Guinness* and can then enjoy the best all-round view of the city. *Daily 9.30am–5pm, July–Aug until 7pm | admission fee 13.50 euro | St James's Gate | www.guinness-storehouse.com | bus: 51B, 78A from Aston Quay, 123 from O'Connell St. and Dame St.*

## IRISH MUSEUM OF MODERN ART 🌿
**(111 E6) (*ⅅ* D5)**

The national collection of modern art is kept in Kilmainham in the imposing old Royal Hospital, once a home for war veterans. The museum has been collecting artworks since 1990 and has some top quality temporary exhibitions. The museum lies on a hill with a view on to the river and a beautiful garden in the style of the 18th century. The café and art bookstore are also recommended. *Tue–Sat 10am–5.30pm, Sun midday–5.30pm | free admission | www.imma.ie | 5 min on foot from Heuston Station, from there with Luas line 1 and buses 51, 79 from Aston Quay*

## KILMAINHAM GAOL ★ ●
**(111 E–F6) (*ⅅ* D5)**

To the Irish a visit to the 200-year-old prison is a patriotic pilgrimage while for the foreign visitor it is an interesting history lesson. Volunteers were responsible for the building's restoration and the re-opening of Kilmainham Gaol, which is a monument to the country's history. It includes the old prison wing that was in operation in 1796 and an extension from the 1860s. The tour is highly informative and you will learn a lot about the theory and practice of the penal system as well as the rehabilitation of criminals – an interesting topic especially when you are standing in the dank cells yourself. The primary focus is on the leaders of the 1916 Easter Rising, who were executed at Kilmainham Gaol. The adjacent exhibition gives you a good overview of the Irish struggle for independence from 1798–

1922. *April–Sept daily 9.30am–6pm, Oct–March Mon–Sat 9.30am–5.30pm, Sun 10am–6pm | admission fee 6 euro | Inchicore Road | www.heritageireland.ie | bus: 51B, 78A, 79, 79A from Aston Quay*

## NATIONAL BOTANIC GARDENS ●
**(112 B2) (*ⅅ* F2)**

The 200-year-old botanical garden is a wonderful place to retreat to when Dublin's busy traffic becomes too much. Exotic floral species from all over the world thrive in a protected valley at the Tolka River where palm trees and orchids grow in elegant old greenhouses. *Nov–Feb daily 9am–4.30pm, March–Oct Mon–Fri 9am–5pm, Sat/Sun 10am–6pm | free admission | Botanic Road | www.botanicgardens.ie | bus: 13, 13A and 19 from O'Connell St.*

## PHOENIX PARK ★ ● 🌿
**(110–111 A–E 1–5) (*ⅅ* A–D 1–4)**

After a night of partying in Temple Bar the fresh air of Phoenix Park, and the views of the Wicklow Mountains, are an ideal way to clear the mind. Dublin's equivalent of the green Irish countryside was once the royal red deer reserve. Today Phoenix Park also accommodates sports meetings and other big events. 120,000 guests attended the Robbie Williams concert but Pope John Paul II attracted the largest crowd, an estimated 1.2 million, in 1979. At the entrance is an obelisk that honours Wellington's victory at Waterloo, north-west from there is the head of state's residence, right in the centre of the park. The *Dublin Zoo*, where the famous MGM lion was born, is situated in the east of the park. *Park open all day every day | Zoo Mon–Sat 9.30am–6pm, Sun 10.30am–6pm (admission fee 15 euro, children 10.50 euro) | bus: 25, 25A, 26, 66, 67 from Wellington Quay | Luas: Museum or Heuston, then about 10 min on foot*

# WHERE TO GO

### DUN LAOGHAIRE/KILLINEY/ SANDYCOVE (117 F5) *(∅ 0)*

You can visit other places of interest on the coast south of the capital by taking the city's urban railway, the ● DART. The *James Joyce Museum*, housed in the Martello Tower *(April–Aug Tue–Sat 10am–5pm, Sun 2pm–4pm | admission fee 6 euro | www.dun-laoghaire.com)* in *Sandycove* is a cultural highlight on this stretch of coast. If you haven't read his opus then **INSIDER TIP** take 'Ulysses' with you and read the first chapter on the turret roof, as this is where it plays out. If the book does not captivate you here on site then it never will! The highlight – literally – is the ※ *Killiney Hill summit* with wonderful views over the coast and mountains. A number of restaurants in *Dun Laoghaire* or Sandycove sell refreshments, for the more daring the cold water of the Irish Sea awaits at the *Forty Foot* bathing area. The trip with the DART from Connolly Station to Dun Laoghaire takes 25 min, 35 min to Killiney.

### HOWTH (117 F4) *(∅ 0)*

There are many reasons why the village of Howth, which lies north-east of Dublin on a peninsula, is such a popular tourist destination: its beautiful town centre, good seafood restaurants, the hustle and bustle of the harbour, the fresh sea air on a boat trip and the wonderful cliff walks. The trip with the DART from Connolly Station takes 24 min. A bit slower, but scenically far more beautiful, is the **INSIDER TIP** bus trip with panoramic view from the top deck, line 31 B from Eden Quay or Connolly Station.

Why not take a day trip out of Dublin to pretty Killiney Bay

# FOOD & DRINK

The ingredients are top quality: Irish waters supply oysters, prawns and fresh fish, while lush green meadows provide tender beef and lamb. Yet Ireland's culinary tradition was once as poor as its population. Those days are long gone: Dubliners are wealthier now and can afford to go to decent restaurants. Immigrants from all over the world brought their culinary specialities to the Emerald Isle and as local chefs eventually discovered the French, Asian and Mediterranean art of preparing and seasoning high quality local ingredients, 'modern Irish cuisine' was born.

The down side of this was the price hike and despite the recession, Dublin is still one of the most expensive cities in Europe, especially when it comes to restaurants. There are however still some ways to save money and there are a wealth of cafés and pubs that offer inexpensive lunches. The INSIDER TIP pre-theatre menu is an early bird special that makes fine dining accessible in the evenings: patrons arriving from about 6pm can order two to three courses at a set price, but have to leave by 8pm. The lunch menus at many places offer people with an ordinary income the chance to experience some fine dining in the best locations but at reasonable prices. Dublin's restaurants generally serve lunch between midday and 2pm,

Photo: Irish Breakfast

Between Irish stew and haute cuisine: Dublin's cuisine has been modern for quite some time, but traditional Irish meals are also served

dinner from about 6.30pm until 10pm, sometimes until 11pm. Most of the pubs open as early as 11am and close at 11.30pm during the week and between 12.30am and 1.30am on Fridays and Saturdays. Modern Dubliners prefer international cuisine to their own traditional meals. If you would like to try Irish stew, bangers and mash or colcannon then the local pubs usually offer some good, hearty tradition-al home-cooking. Pubs like the *Porterhouse*, *The Stag's Head* or *O'Shea's Merchant*, are a better (and far less expensive) alterna-tive to mediocre restaurants. In pubs you usually place your food order at the bar counter. Some restaurants also have a seating system so in those you may need to wait to be seated. Also check if a 'ser-vice charge' is noted on the menu. If the surcharge for the service is not included,

Bewley's Café : coffee chain downstairs or a more dignified tearoom upstairs

and you are happy with the service, then a ten percent tip is appropriate.

The area around Temple Bar is full of all kinds of different restaurants and pubs of varying quality. North of Dame Street there lots of tempting restaurants between Grafton Street and South Great George's Street while the more exclusive restaurants are around Merrion Square and St Stephen's Green. If you love fish and seafood, a trip to the coast at Howth or Sandycove is highly recommended.

## CAFÉS

### AVOCA (109 D4) *(💷 G5)*

The designer shop Avoca with its grocery store and café represents the modern Irish lifestyle. Quiches, tasty soups and the INSIDER TIP enticing smells from its bakery are irresistible and lure in both passersby and the local office workers from the surrounding streets. If you go there before or after lunchtime you will be able to enjoy a good cup of coffee and

a bite to eat without a reservation. *Closed in the evenings | 11 Suffolk St. | tel. 01 6 72 60 19 | bus: Dame St.*

### BEWLEY'S CAFÉ 😊 (109 D5) *(💷 G5)*

Its Egyptian-looking façade conceals a branch of *Café Bar Deli* on the ground floor while on the first floor, breakfast (from 8am) and afternoon teas are served in a comfortable atmosphere with crystal chandeliers, dark wood and old photos. In the *Oriental Room* there are theatre performances during the day, jazz and cabaret in the evenings. *78 Grafton St. | bus: Nassau St.*

### THE CHURCH ★ (108 B3) *(💷 F4)*

A converted 18th century church is the setting for this Northside restaurant with its wooden panelling, commemorative plaques, organ and glass paintings. The impressive interior gives it a great ambience so it's a good choice for a cappuccino, toasted sandwich or a light snack during the day. In the evenings the old

St Mary's Church turns into a trendy club with restaurant and chill-out area and a spacious terrace *(the steaks are a must | Moderate–Expensive)*. *Mary St. | tel. 01 8 28 01 02 | www.thechurch.ie | Luas: Jervis*

### INSIDER TIP COBALT CAFÉ
**(109 D1) (∅ G4)**

This stylish and arty café is a great option for a relaxing and inexpensive lunch on the Northside. It takes up two rooms in a lovely Georgian house with high stucco ceilings. The family-run business serves open baguettes and ciabatta, soups and salads. In winter there is a fire going, while in the summer the sun shines on to the garden tables. *Closed Sundays and evenings | 16 North Great George's St. | bus: Parnell Square*

### QUEEN OF TARTS ★ (108 B4) (∅ F5)

The tempting fare on offer in this cosy café means that it certainly lives up to its claim to being the 'queen of tarts'. Choose between muffins, raspberry cheesecake or plum tarts with your tea or coffee. At lunchtime they also serve soups and small, hot meals. Their wonderful selection of cakes can also be found at a branch around the corner in 3–4 Cow's Lane. *Closed in the evenings | 4 Cork Hill | Lord Edward St. | bus: Lord Edward St.*

## RESTAURANTS: EXPENSIVE

### BANG (109 E6) (∅ G5)

The stylish and beautiful Dublin in-crowd love this fine-dining minimalist restaurant, which serves modern Irish cuisine: besides their refined version of bangers and mash there is also foie gras or gravlax and Irish seafood deliciously combined with ingredients from the Mediterranean or the Orient. *Closed Sundays | 11 Merrion Row | tel. 01 6 76 08 98 | www.bangrestaurant. com | Luas: St Stephen's Green*

### KING SITRIC �◡ (117 F4) (∅ 0)

The Viking King Sitric would certainly not have dined as finely as the guests at this seafood restaurant on Howth harbour where you can enjoy wonderful sea views from the light and bright dining area on the first floor. The menu does have beef and chicken dishes, but it would be a real shame not to order the seafood as everything is freshly caught. Besides lobsters and oysters, turbot and Dublin Bay prawns are also served. For dessert the Irish cheese platter is highly recommended. *Closed Tuesdays, lunch only Sundays | East Pier | Howth | tel. 01 8 32 52 35 | www.kingsitric. ie | DART: Howth*

---

## MARCO POLO HIGHLIGHTS

★ **The Church**
Café in a converted old church – in the evenings it turns into a trendy club and restaurant
→ p. 54

★ **Queen of Tarts**
Tempting tarts and delicious treats near Dublin Castle
→ p. 55

★ **Restaurant 101 Talbot**
Irish and Mediterranean cuisine in a relaxed atmosphere → p. 57

★ **Chapter One**
The perfect showcase for contemporary Irish cuisine → p. 58

★ **Yamamori Noodles**
Asian noodle dishes – healthy and delicious → p. 59

★ **Dunne and Crescenzi**
Enjoy some reasonably priced and tasty Italian fare in amongst the groceries → p. 59

Opulent interior, exquisite wines and creative cuisine – Peploe's Wine Bistro

### MV CILL AIRNE (115 E1) *(𝄐 H4)*

A decommissioned training ship houses the *Quay 16 Restaurant*, the *Blue River Bistro Bar* and the *White Bar*. The kitchen serves contemporary European dishes, primarily meat and fish, with vegetarian meals being the exception. The pre-theatre menu (until 7pm) is inexpensive: three courses cost 25 euro. There is a smart casual dress code and casual wear is not permitted. For safety reasons children are not allowed on board. *Quay 16 | North Wall Quay | tel. 014 45 09 94 | www.mvcillairne.com | Luas: Spencer Dock*

### MARTELLO RESTAURANT (117 F5) *(𝄐 0)*

A popular venue with the residents of the surrounding residential areas but its location, on the promenade between Dun Laoghaire and Sandycove, is also easily accessible to tourists. The committed team prepares fresh Irish ingredients like lamb, sole or Dublin Bay crab meat with French flair and verve and serves good wines go with them. *1 Martello Terrace | Sandycove | tel. 01 2 80 98 71 | DART: Sandycove*

### PEPLOE'S WINE BISTRO (109 D6) *(𝄐 G5)*

This chic bar and restaurant, in an opulently furnished basement, is in an excellent location. It is principally a wine bar with a wide selection of fine wines from Europe and the southern hemisphere. But Peploe's is also a good choice for their modern, creative cuisine where the lamb, game and seafood dishes have strong Mediterranean influences. *Closed Sun | 16 St Stephen's Green | tel. 01 6 76 31 44 | www.peploes.com | Luas: St Stephen's Green*

### IL BACCARO (108 C4) *(𝄐 F5)*

Osteria – wine tavern – is the right definition for this bit of Italy in the middle of Temple Bar. Two low brick vaulted ceilings create the atmospheric framework for their simple Italian cuisine. Pasta, simple country food like lamb with chickpeas and classics like saltimbocca are served in a friendly atmosphere – and their house wine is not only good but also affordable.

*Meeting House Square | tel. 01 6 71 45 97 | bus: Temple Bar*

**INSIDER TIP BAR ITALIA** (108 C3) *(∅ F5)*
This is a good choice for some delicious and authentic Italian cuisine – the minestrone is as remarkable as the gnocchi and you will be hard pressed to find a better espresso in Dublin. And they also have live broadcasts when Italy plays football. *26 Lower Ormond Quay | tel. 01 8 74 10 00 | www.baritalia.ie | bus: Ormond Quay, Luas: Jervis Street*

### FITZERS (108 C4) *(∅ G5)*
International cuisine that covers the range from burgers and chips, steaks and roast lamb from Wicklow through to pasta and fish. Simple and modern cuisine with a great ambience in converted warehouse. *43 Temple Bar Square | tel. 01 6 79 04 40 | www.fitzers.ie | bus: Temple Bar*

### HARBOURMASTER (109 F2) *(∅ G4)*
A pub and restaurant – in what was once the harbour master's office in the Docklands – that is a popular choice with workers from the surrounding finance district. The atmospheric building, with its wooden benches and rough brick, houses a pub that serves simple dishes while the chic extension building serves up international cuisine with Irish influences. *Custom House Dock | tel. 01 G 70 16 88 | Luas: Connolly Station*

### LORD EDWARD'S SEAFOOD RESTAURANT (108 B4) *(∅ F5)*
The well-established Dublin restaurant is on the floor above a pub of the same name. It uses good quality ingredients for tried and tested fresh seafood classics like plaice and sole, scallops and turbot or sometimes lobster (if you want to reach a bit deeper into your wallet). Conveniently situated near the cathedrals – for a more upmarket lunch. *Closed for lunch Sat and Sun | Christchurch Place | tel. 01 4 54 24 20 | bus: Lord Edward St.*

### RESTAURANT 101 TALBOT ★ (109 D2) *(∅ G4)*
Besides classic Italian pasta dishes you can also order Irish beef here. Fresh fish from local waters is prepared and served in Mediterranean style, e.g. halibut with *salsa verde* and for vegetarians there is a selection of meals like wild mushroom risotto. Due to its location – in the shopping area around O'Connell and near to the Abbey and the Gate Theatre – 101 Talbot is usually already quite full by early evening. *Closed Sun, Mon, Pre-Theatre Menu from*

# LOW BUDGET

▶ Reasonably priced Chinese restaurants can be found in Dublin's growing Chinatown on Parnell Street in the section east of Parnell Square and on Chapel Street.

▶ Why not go the self-catering route and go shopping in the supermarkets in the Jervis Centre and *ILAC Centre* **(108 C2–3)** *(∅ F4)* or one of the small Spar shops and then have a picnic in one of Dublin's beautiful parks.

▶ Many pubs serve meals from midday until early evening, they range from soups to roast beef with all the trimmings. The portions are plentiful and the prices (by Dublin's standards) are really reasonable. An excellent option is *The Brian Boru* **(112 B3)** *(∅ F2)* near the Glasnevin Cemetery. *9 Prospect Road | www.thebrianboru. ie | bus 4, 13, 19, 19a: Hart's Corner*

*5pm | 101 Talbot St. | tel. 01 8 74 50 11 | www.101talbot.com | Luas: Abbey St.*

### `INSIDER TIP` SHEEBEN CHIC
(108 C4) (*F5*)

Restaurant and bar on two floors with some funky and unusual décor. There is always something going on in this place, whether it is a traditional music session or a flea market – which is why it can be a bit loud at times. *Daily 4pm–midnight | 4 South Great Georges St. | tel. 01 6 79 96 67 | bus: Dame Street*

### THE WINDING STAIR ☺
(108 C3) (*F5*)

If you knew this place as a bookstore and café, you might be a bit heart sore at the sight of the new chic restaurant and small bookstore. But the gourmets will enjoy it all the more for the contemporary and organic Irish fine-dining cuisine that is now being served here. Indulge in the delicious Irish mussels or the charcuterie plate or trout from Lough Neagh. Depending on choice the starter and main meal cost about 35 euro. *40 Lower Ormond Quay |*

# GOURMET RESTAURANTS

### Chapter One ⭐ (108 C1) (*F4*)

The much-acclaimed representative of 'modern Irish cooking' is located in the *Dublin Writers Museum*. Serving delicious dishes like their charcuterie platter (using only Irish suppliers), lobster-filled ravioli and local *Aberdeen Angus* steak with mushroom gratin. A three course meal in the early evening costs 37.50, main meals à la carte from 30 euro. *Closed Sun, Mon | 18 Parnell Square | tel. 01 8 73 22 66 | www.chapterone restaurant.com | bus: Parnell Square*

### L'Écrivain (109 F6) (*G6*)

Irishman Derry Clark has consistently held on to his well-deserved Michelin award. He uses fresh local ingredients and creative sauces and side dishes to conjure up a fine dining experience, and his meals regularly receive high praise from Dublin's food critics. Main meals à la carte cost about 40 euro, the seven course tasting menu is about 95 euro. *Closed Sun, Sat lunchtime | 109 a Lower Baggot St. | tel. 01 6 61 19 19 | www. lecrivain.com | bus: Merrion Square*

### Restaurant Patrick Guilbaud
(109 E6) (*G5*)

The elegant *Merrion Hotel* is the perfect setting for two star Michelin chef Guilbaud's French *haute cuisine*. At lunchtime there are two courses for 38 euro, but in the evenings the starter and main meal cost about 50 euro more. For such impeccable dining you will need to be impeccably dressed! *Closed Sun, Mon | 21 Upper Merrion St. | tel. 01 6 76 41 92 | www.restaurantpatrick guilbaud.ie | Luas: St Stephen's Green*

### The Tea Room (108 C3) (*F5*)

This celebrity hang out, in the elegant *Clarence Hotel,* serves up traditional Irish ingredients in a very contemporary way but the fine dining menu doesn't mean that the atmosphere is stiff. It is actually light, airy and – like the meals – simple rather than overdone. The cheapest is the three course 'Market Menu' for 23 euro, main meals à la carte cost about 12–30 euro. *Essex St. | tel. 01 4 07 08 13 | www.theclarence.ie | bus: Temple Bar*

*tel. 01 8 72 73 20 | www.winding-stair.com | bus: Ormond Quay, Luas: Abbey St.*

## YAMAMORI NOODLES ★
**(108 C4) (꧅ F5)**

Healthy Japanese noodle dishes, soups, and sushi and a stylish interior. This is also a good option for vegetarians or those wanting to grab a bite before setting off on a pub crawl in the area north of Dame Street. *71/72 South Great George's St. | tel. 01 4 75 50 01 | www.yamamorinoodles.ie | bus: South Great George's St.*; another branch is *Yamamori Sushi* **(108 C3) (꧅ F5)** | *38/39 Lower Ormond Quay | tel. 01 8 72 00 03 | Luas: Abbey St.*

## RESTAURANTS: BUDGET

### BESHOFF'S ✲ (109 D2) (꧅ G4)

There are those who think that Leo Burdock's fish and chips are a bit better, but Beshoff's has also been a real Dublin institute for centuries. It has a great view from the first floor on to the busy hustle and bustle of O'Connell Street down below. The interior is surprising: classical pillars, colourful stained glass windows and comfortable seats all create a surprisingly up-market ambience for a fish and chip shop. *6 O'Connell St. Upper | bus: O'Connell St. | another branch at 14 Westmoreland St. near Trinity College*

### CORNUCOPIA ☺ (109 D4) (꧅ G5)

One of the oldest vegetarian restaurants in Dublin and vegans and those with yeast, dairy, gluten or nut allergies will be able to order delicious meals and feel right at home here. *19 Wicklow St. | tel. 01 6 77 75 83 | www.cornucopia.ie | bus: Dame St.*

### DUNNE AND CRESCENZI ★
**(109 D5) (꧅ G5)**

Italian flair, good quality food, reasonable prices and its position near Trinity College

and Grafton Street all make for a recipe for success for this wine, grocery store and restaurant. The menu is not extensive, but there is a selection of antipasti, *Panini*

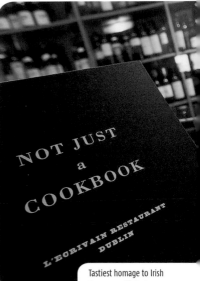

Tastiest homage to Irish literature: L'Écrivain

and small dishes that vary daily. Inside you are seated between shelves full of Italian wine and pasta, and you can enjoy some sun and a glass of Prosecco at the tables in the front. *16 South Frederick St. | Tel 01 6 77 38 15 | bus: Nassau St.*

### GALLAGHER'S BOXTY HOUSE
**(108 C3) (꧅ G5)**

Favourite address for fans of the Emerald Isle's traditional cuisine, and its comfortable traditional Irish atmosphere makes it a great place for you to discover the tastes of colcannon, coddle and boxty pancakes. The pancakes have a variety of rich and hearty fillings. *20 Temple Bar | tel. 01 6 77 27 62 | www.boxtyhouse.ie | bus: Temple Bar*

# LOCAL SPECIALITIES

▶ **Bangers and mash** – typical pub meal of grilled sausages with mashed potatoes (photo left)

▶ **Boxty** – pancakes made using a mixture of potatoes, flour and either buttermilk, egg or butter

▶ **Coddle** – a casserole of potatoes, onions, bacon and sausage

▶ **Colcannon** – mashed potatoes with cabbage, milk, cream, leeks or onions

▶ **Fish and chips** – this may be the English national dish, but the Irish have put their patriotism aside and love their battered and fried fish fillet with salt and vinegar chips

▶ **Irish breakfast** – the full version includes fruit juice, cornflakes or muesli, scrambled eggs, fried bacon and sausage, black and white pudding (blood and liver sausage), baked beans and tomatoes, finished off with plenty of toast with jam; you get strong tea with it, coffee only on request. Eat one of these and you won't need lunch

▶ **Irish stew** – casserole of lamb with potatoes, carrots and onions

▶ **Pie** – pies are an Irish staple: try a classic fish pie and then round it off with a slice of apple pie (photo right)

▶ **Stout** – dark top-fermented beer, like Guinness or Murphy's

▶ **Whiskey** – the Irish kind often tastes smoother than the Scottish. The most famous brands are Jameson and Bushmills and their characteristic flavour and quality are still as good as ever. There are also many other small producers.

**INSIDER TIP JUICE**
(108 C4) (*ᗅ F5*)

Serves healthy and tasty vegetarian dishes from all over the world – like *frittata*, Thai curry or Moroccan tagine – and in comparison to other Dublin restaurants, the prices are very reasonable. The setting is also attractively simple and contemporary. Try the early bird menu, a three-course meal for 14.95 euro *(Mon–Fri 5pm–7pm)* and enjoy one of their unusual fruit and vegetable juice combinations. *73 South Great George's Street | tel. 01 4 75 78 56 | www.juicerestaurant.ie | bus: South Great George's St.*

**LEO BURDOCK'S** ●
(108 B4) (*ᗅ F5*)

Fish and chips fans argue about which establishment is the best but when it comes to celebrity clients, this small shop near Christ Church Cathedral wins hands down. A large board next to the shop entrance lists some of its world-famous clients: Sinead O'Connor, Rod Stewart, Tom Cruise, Sandra Bullock and many more. The generous portions can be bought as a take away and then enjoyed on a nearby bench in Dublin Castle gardens or in front of the cathedral. *2 Werburgh St. | bus: Lord Edward St.*

### INSIDER TIP  LOUIE'S BISTRO ☺
(112–113 C–D4) (*ill* G3)

This restaurant, in the basement of a beautifully renovated Georgian townhouse, might not be situated in the best area of Dublin but it is worth a visit. The chef values organic Irish products so the meat is certified which means delicious options like the slow cooked pork belly stew. There are usually at least three fish dishes as well as some vegetarian options. At the end of the dining room, a flight of stairs leads to a lounge with comfortable seating ideal for an after dinner drink, and on the terrace behind the glass door is a smoking section in the garden. They also have an early bird special (order before 7pm) which is a three course meal for 25 euro or 65 euro (for two) including a bottle of wine. *Daily midday–3pm, Wed–Sat 5pm–11pm | 20 Mountjoy Square East | tel. 01 8 36 45 88 | www.louies.ie | bus: Mountjoy Square*

### INSIDER TIP  MARKET BAR
(108 C5) (*ill* F5)

Behind an unassuming façade lies one of the most stylish bars in Dublin. A café by day, a tapas bar by night or simply a hip and happening place to enjoy a glass of wine. What was once a market hall and sausage factory has been converted into an airy space with rustic benches under a high vaulted glass and iron ceiling. The lack of music – very unusual in Dublin! – means an evening of conversation and *craic*. The wine list includes a good selection from Spain and South America. *Fade St. | tel. 01 6 13 90 94 | www.marketbar.ie | bus: South Great George's St.*

Catch the early bird vegetarian menu for less than 15 euro at Juice

# SHOPPING

Photo: St Stephen's Green Centre

**WHERE TO START?**
(109 D4–5) *(∭ G5)* **Grafton Street:** The best parts of this elegant shopping street are in the pedestrian zone and in the adjacent streets to the west up to South Great George's Street and in the east up to Kildare Street. Ideal for high quality fashion, art and jewellery, books and CDs, souvenirs and groceries. *Luas: St Stephen's Green/bus 90, 92, 93*

A shopping trip is always fun and in Dublin it is even more so because its main shopping area, south of the Liffey, is very compact with everything in easy walking distance.

A few minutes walk away from Grafton Street are the small trendy designer shops of Temple Bar. If you would rather not spend a lot of money then cross over the Liffey and take a wander around the side streets off O'Connell Street where you are bound to find something suitable. Here is where you will find some large shopping malls with branches of all the big chain stores and department stores. In Earl Street, which leads off O'Connell Street near the Spire, you will find a row of shops which all sell inexpensive every-

So much for Celtic kitsch: discover how stylish, tasteful and beautifully creative the Irish can really be

day clothing and cheap Asian imports. Only those on the lookout for some special antiques will have to head out of the city centre and go towards Francis Street in the Liberties. And for book lovers there is Dawson Street and *Hodges Figgis bookstore* (mentioned by James Joyce) as well as a number of other smaller book shops, which have each chosen a particular specialty like detective stories or rare books.

Apropos prices: they differ widely in Dublin, so you should avoid impulse buying and first shop around and compare prices. Especially CDs and DVDs (but also for clothing and souvenirs) which are available on every street corner in the centre and also in the INSIDERTIP museum shops. Whiskey lovers are better off buying their favourite tipple at home: most Irish whiskeys cost more in Ireland than they do elsewhere.

# BOOKS

Powerscourt Centre: from elegant Georgian townhouse to exclusive shopping centre

## BOOKS

### CHAPTER'S (108 C2) (*m F4*)
This independent bookstore includes a large second-hand book section, where you can pick up some real finds, they also sell CDs and DVDs. If you are looking for cheap books by famous (or not so famous) Irish writers then this will be the best place for you. The personnel are also exceptionally friendly and very helpful. *Ivy Exchange, Parnell Street | Luas: Jervis*

### HODGES FIGGIS (109 D5) (*m G5*)
This well-established and well-stocked bookstore – in the area north of Trinity College, where many other bookshops are located – is highly recommended for Irish authors and literature. *56–58 Dawson St. | bus: Nassau St.*

## SHOPPING CENTRES

### ILAC CENTRE AND JERVIS CENTRE (108 C2–3) (*m F4*)
These two shopping centres are located very near to each other in the pedestrian zone west of O'Connell Street, there is little that separates them in terms of shopping as the large British chains like Marks and Spencer, Next and Debenhams dominate them both. There are no small individual shops here, but everything is under one roof. *Henry St. | Luas: Jervis*

### POWERSCOURT CENTRE ★ (109 D5) (*m G5*)
An 18th century aristocratic city residence has been converted into sophisticated and exclusive shopping area selling interesting items and antiques such as clocks, silver or porcelain figurines, ball and wedding gowns, shoes and toys. The *Pygmalion Café* in the covered courtyard is the ideal place to take a rest from your shopping and to sit back and enjoy a cup of coffee and a slice of cake or a light lunch. *59 William St. South | bus: Dame St.*

### ST STEPHEN'S GREEN CENTRE (108 C5–6) (*m G5*)
An ambitious centre that looks like a massive Victorian greenhouse; it has shopping arcades on three floors and is the leading

shopping centre in the south side and especially good for sports gear. The selection of clothing is massive and usually quite inexpensive, but not very unique. *St Stephen's Green West | Luas: St Stephen's Green*

## GROCERIES

**FALLON AND BYRNE** (108 C4) (*ɰ F5*)
This establishment has the sort of clientele who want superior quality groceries, ones that list the provenance of the items. Fruit and vegetables, fish and meat, cheese, pastries as well as fine wines can be purchased here or enjoyed in-house at the Brasserie Restaurant. *11 Exchequer St. | bus: South Great George's St.*

**MAGILL'S** (109 D5) (*ɰ G5*)
Delicatessen that caters to every culinary wish, the Condon family offers bread from Wicklow, cheeses and meats from all regions of Ireland, home-made salads, exquisite olive oil and lots more. *14 Clarendon Street | bus: South Great George's St.*

**SHERIDAN'S CHEESE SHOP**
(109 D5) (*ɰ G5*)
Ireland's lush meadows and pastures yield first class cheeses and Sheridan's offers INSIDER TIP handmade specialities from Irish farms. Try the blue cheese Cashel Blue or the firm Coolea from Cork or simply let the well-informed personnel advise you. *11 Anne St. South | Luas: St Stephen's Green*

## MARKETS

**HONEST2GOODNESS MARKET** ☺
(112 A2) (*ɰ E2*)
Dublin's newest market, in an inconspicuous old warehouse facility, is situated only a few minutes away from the Glasnevin Cemetery. On offer is mostly organic Irish produce like bread, fruit and vegetables,

cheese and meat, but also olive oils, Mediterranean antipasti, organic wines and home-made curry sauces. At lunchtime there are also cooking presentations, so if you'd like to make the demonstrated dish all the ingredients are right on hand here. *Sat 9.30am–4pm | Glasnevin Industrial Estate | 136 a Slaney Close | bus: Finglas Road/Esso filling station*

**MARKET ARCADE** (108 C5) (*ɰ F5*)
The old market hall is a veritable treasure trove of beautiful souvenirs: goldsmith's work and handicrafts, second-hand books and CDs, Asian clothing and stylish second-hand fashion. And the food stalls are top-notch. *Between South Great George's St. and Drury St. | bus: South Great George's St.*

**MOORE STREET MARKET** ●
(108 C2) (*ɰ G4*)
This fruit and vegetable market is often seen as a remnant of old Dublin, however its traditional nature is changing and there

Gourmet delicacies and fresh produce from the Irish countryside: the Temple Bar Food Market

are now traders from the Far East and Eastern Europe. *Moore St. | Luas: Jervis*

### TEMPLE BAR FOOD MARKET ★
(108 C4) *(ØØ F5)*

This small Saturday market has as its focus local Irish produce, much of it organic and there is an especially tempting selection of delicious fresh farmhouse cheeses, smoked fish, handmade pralines, jams, preserves and gourmet sausages. *Sat 10am–5pm | Meeting House Square | bus: Temple Bar*

### AVOCA HANDWEAVERS ★
(109 D4) *(ØØ G5)*

The varied selection and wide range on offer makes this attractive multi-storey shop feel like a department store. Don't miss out on the *Food Hall* in the basement where you can buy all the INSIDER TIP ingredients for a lovely picnic in nearby St Stephen's Green: freshly baked bread, Irish cheeses, pies, tapas or sushi. On the ground floor there is contemporary Irish fashion and household goods. If there is no more space in the café on the top floor, simply buy the Avoca cookbook and try out the dishes yourself. *11 Suffolk St. | bus: Dame St.*

### BROWN THOMAS ★ (109 D5) *(ØØ G5)*

This exclusive department store has four floors of fashion for men and women. On the ground floor are brands like Gucci, Hermès, Dior, Prada and Louis Vuitton and the perfume and cosmetics section has absolutely everything the heart desires. *28 Grafton St. | Luas: St Stephen's Green*

### INSIDER TIP COVET – THE BORROWERS BOUDOIR (109 D5) *(ØØ G5)*

It's all in the name and who hasn't coveted something that belongs to someone else? In this shop you can give into temptation. When you shop here you don't have to actually buy the latest garments by international designers like Galliano or Cavalli, instead you can simply hire them – at a fraction (well, at 10 per cent) of the original price. *Powerscourt Centre | 59 William St. South | bus: Dame St.*

### THE FEATHERED MILLINER
(108 C3) (*ᗰ F5*)

Many female Dubliners make their own hats and this shop sells hats and everything that is required for hat-making: feathers, ribbons, millinery wire, silk bands and much more. The shop is an offshoot of the neighbouring *Beads and Bling,* where you can get all the stuff you need to make your own jewellery. *5 Bedford Row | Luas: Jervis*

### HAPPY DAYS ☺ (108 C4) (*ᗰ G5*)

A shopping paradise and not just for old hippies. The shop with its Indian atmosphere sells bags, scarves, dresses, skirts, jewellery, incense and much more and by Dublin standards the items are relatively inexpensive. All the items sold are ethically produced or fair trade products. *2 Crown Alley | bus: Dame Street*

### THE HARLEQUIN (108 C5) (*ᗰ G5*)

The small shop doesn't make much of an impression from the outside, but it is well worth a visit. Vintage clothing, bags, accessories, hats – all retro or used – but be warned, nothing here is cheap. *13 Castle Market | bus: South Great George's St.*

### KENNEDY AND MCSHARRY
(109 D4) (*ᗰ G5*)

Established in 1890, this is Dublin's leading menswear store. The fourth generation family business sells woollen hats and caps – the kind that an Irish gentleman would wear – conservative but stylish. In addition they also have a great selection of raincoats, tweed jackets and shirts. *37 Nassau St. | bus: Nassau St.*

### THE SWOPSHOP ☺ (108 C4) (*ᗰ F5*)

Designer fashion with a difference: the goods are used, and you can swop some of your own clothing as payment – but on condition that they are still cool and trendy. Upgrade your wardrobe and do your bit for the environment at the same time! At the Swopshop you can find labels from Prada to Principles, but also tailor-made pieces and you can trade in your accessories. *Crow Street Bazaar | 7 Crow St. | bus: Dame Street*

### WILD CHILD ORIGINALS
(108 C4) (*ᗰ F5*)

While the major department stores copy the vintage clothing trend, here you can get the originals. The shop always has

## LOW BUDGET

▶ If you want to save money, then do your shopping north of the Liffey. Department stores like *Dunne's* on Henry Street sell clothing at reasonable prices while the neighbouring *Moore Street Market* is a good choice for groceries.

▶ Second-hand books, CDs, clothing and more can always be found in the local charity shops, several of them are in the area in and around Capel Street while second-hand books can be found at *Oxfam Books (25 Parliament Street).*

▶ There is also the weekend market in the suburb of *Blackrock* (117 E5) (*ᗰ 0*) on the coast south of the city. Not everything is cheap, but if you hunt around you will find some bargains: clothing, accessories, furniture and esoteric bric-a-brac. *Main Street | Blackrock | Sat 11am–5.30pm, Sun 10am–5.30pm | DART: Blackrock*

# MUSIC

specials, sometimes offering three items for the price of two or they sell items according to weight: a kilo costs 20 euro. For that weight you could get five summer dresses or some T-shirts or three jackets ... *26 Drury St. | bus: South Great George's St.*

## MUSIC

**CLADDAGH RECORDS** (108 C4) *(∅ F5)*
Founded over 50 years ago to promote traditional Irish music, Claddagh Records is still one of the leading shops for Celtic music. *2 Cecilia St. | bus: Temple Bar*

**INSIDER TIP MOJO RECORDS**
(108 C3) *(∅ G5)*
At the end of Ha'penny Bridge under the *Merchants Arch* is a small bit of a paradise for music lovers. In this tiny record store you will find all those records that have been on your wish list for years – whether CD or vinyl. There are also DVDs, music posters and memorabilia. Mojo Records specialises in Irish rock. On the upper floor there is a small section with second-hand books. *4 Merchants Arch | Temple Bar | bus: Ormond Quay*

**WALTON'S WORLD OF MUSIC**
(108 C5) *(∅ F5)*
If you would like to play traditional Irish music yourself or are looking for a special gift, then this place is a must. In this charmingly old-fashioned shop you can buy yourself a traditional Irish drum *(bodhran)* or a small tin whistle. *69 South Great George's St. | bus: South Great George's St.*

# BOOKS & FILMS

▶ **Dubliners** – James Joyce's portrait of the city 100 years ago – easier to read than his older works, such as 'Ulysses'. The latter had a profound influence on 20th century literature and immortalised the city of Dublin. It is a challenging read, but those who read it look at the city – and perhaps life – from a new perspective

▶ **Speckled People** – Hugo Hamilton's mother was a German emigrant, his father a staunch Irish nationalist whose children were only allowed to speak Gaelic or German but not English. Hamilton's best-selling memoir movingly describes his culturally confused Dublin childhood (2004)

▶ **Dublin 4** – By popular Irish author Maeve Binchy, it is a book of four charming and entertaining short stories about the everyday lives of residents from this post code area in Dublin (1978)

▶ **The Barrytown Trilogy** – Whether as a screenplay or a book, Roddy Doyle's trilogy is both thought-provoking and highly entertaining. *The Commitments, Fish & Chips* and *The Snapper* play out in Dublin's poor housing estates. Humorous and compassionate, the Doyle depicts the triumphs and failures of his own folk in their daily fight for survival. The film version of *The Commitments* (1991) by Alan Parker has achieved cult status

▶ **McCarthy's Bar – A Journey of Discovery in Ireland** – A hugely entertaining account of travel writer Pete McCarthy's trip around his mother's homeland. Full of hilarious adventures and off beat anecdotes (1999)

Last minute souvenir shopping: House of Ireland also has a branch at the airport

## JEWELLERY

**NEW MOON** (108 C5) (*∅ F5*)
A rather unique jewellery store that sells not only their own handcrafted designs but also traditional and exotic gemstones (amber, amethyst, emerald, garnet, jasper, lapis lazuli, opal, ruby, moonstone and much more) as well as ethnic Eastern jewellery. *George's Street Arcade | 28 Drury Street | bus: South Great George's St.*

**RHINESTONES** (109 D4) (*∅ G5*)
Specialists in antique and costume jewellery. Don't be discouraged by the prices as the friendly employees are always willing to negotiate. *18 St Andrew's St. | bus: Trinity St.*

## SHOES

**CHINA BLUE** (108 C3) (*∅ G5*)
Under the *Merchants Arch*, at the entrance to Temple Bar on the Liffey riverbank, is where you will find this shoe shop selling every make and brand from Gola, Caterpillar, Ben Sherman, Pepe through to Converse. They have the full spectrum of styles from chunky Doc Martens through to elegant Chinese silk slippers – even handmade cowboy boots from Venezuela. *14 Merchants Arch | Temple Bar | bus: Ormond Quay*

## SOUVENIRS

**HOUSE OF IRELAND**
(109 D4) (*∅ G5*)
This establishment sells a broad range of excellent quality Irish products. In addition to classic Waterford crystal glassware, tableware and lamps they also sell ladies' fashion, warm Aran pullovers, Irish linen bedding and tablecloths, Celtic jewellery and carved chess pieces. *Corner Nassau St. /Dawson St. | bus: Nassau St., also at the airport*

**KILKENNY SHOP**
(109 D4) (*∅ G5*)
Clothing, jewellery and bags by young local designers make this shop more stylish than most of the places that sell more traditional Irish items. Also good handicrafts. *6 Nassau St. | bus: Nassau St.*

**THE TEMPLE BAR TRADING COMPANY**
(108 C4) (*∅ F5*)
Right next to *The Temple Bar* pub, this multi-storey establishment is full of souvenirs and gifts to suit all tastes. On the ground floor they sell Dublin logo clothing while on the top floor there are Guinness and Jameson souvenirs. You can also buy rugby jerseys, pub signs, books, Irish music, local art and much more. *43/44 Temple Bar | bus: Dame Street*

# ENTERTAINMENT

**CITY WHERE TO START?**
(108 C4) (*M* F–G5) Temple Bar: This is where you will find all the bars, pubs, restaurants and night clubs. The area between the Liffey and Dame Street, with its cobble-stoned alleyways might be geared toward tourists, but it is also a firm favourite amongst locals and Dublin's youth. *Luas: Jervis/bus: An Lár*

**The nightlife and the music scene are, for many, one of the main reasons for a visit to Dublin. Whether you like traditional Irish music in a typical old pub or prefer stylish designer bars or like to stay up all night dancing to the latest sounds: this vibrant city will not disappoint.**

Nobody really knows how many pubs Dublin has, 800? 1000? Whatever the figure, it is certainly enough to cater to everyone's taste, and enough to need some sort of a guide to help orientate you. Trendier than Temple Bar is the scene in the narrow alleys south of Dame Street, around Dame Lane and Exchequer Street while over on the north side of the Liffey at Ormond Quay, and its side streets, theme pubs attract a young clientele but in both areas bouncers are always present.

**Whether you want to paint the town red or relax and take it easy – anything goes! Dublin is as colourful by night as it is by day**

They are there to bar the way for those who have had too much to drink and – in the smarter clubs – those who are inappropriately dressed. Traditional pubs are spread across the entire inner city with a concentration in Merrion Row and Baggot Street Lower. As Dublin is a cultural and literary city an evening at the theatre is also highly recommended. And of course there is always a concert taking place some-where in the city whether it be Irish folk music, jazz or rock. Tickets are available at *Ticketmaster | tel. * 0 03 53 14 56 95 69 (from outside of Ireland) or * 08 18 71 93 00 (in Dublin) | www.ticketmaster.ie* or directly at the *Tourist Office* in Suffolk Street. Find out what evening events are on in the free, bimonthly 'Event Guide' *(www.entertain ment.ie)*, online at *www.indublin.ie* and in the monthly paper 'Totally Dublin'.

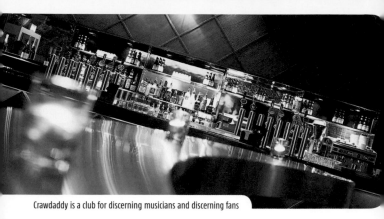

Crawdaddy is a club for discerning musicians and discerning fans

## BARS & CLUBS

**4 DAME LANE** (108 C4) (*∭ G5*)
This bar, with dance floor and good DJs, surprises with its medieval looking wall torches at the entrance, but inside its high brick walls the interior design is minimalist and contemporary. *Mon–Sat until 2.30am, Sun until 1am | 4 Dame Lane | bus: Dame St.*

**DICE BAR** (112 A6) (*∭ E4*)
There has been a pub on this piece of land off Smithfield Square's since 1770. Today the Dice Bar resides here and its black and red décor helps to give it a slight New York vibe. They brew their own beer: *Revolution Red* and there is live music on weekends, otherwise DJs. *Mon–Thu 4pm–11.30pm, Fri/Sat 4pm–0.30am, and Sun 4pm–11pm | www.thatsitdublin.com | 79 Queen St. | Luas: Smithfield*

**OCTAGON BAR** (108 C3) (*∭ G5*)
The octagonal room in the exclusive Clarence Hotel is an oasis of elegant style in the middle of Temple Bar. Owner Bono rarely looks in, but even without him the cocktails taste great and they have draft Guinness at a surprisingly competitive price. *Sun–Wed midday–11.30pm, Thu–Sat 11am–0.30am | 6–8 Wellington Quay | bus: Temple Bar*

**POD** ★ (114 C3) (*∭ G6*)
Dress well so you are sure to make it past the eagle eyes of the bouncers at PoD (Palace of Dance) so you can experience the underground atmosphere on its circular dance floor in the granite vault of an old train station. The club's clever use of lighting and interior design – in reds and oranges – has a lot to do with the catacomb-like mood. *Wed–Sat 11pm–2.20am | Harcourt St. | www.pod.ie | Luas: Harcourt St.*

## BINGO

● Bingo is played more passionately in Ireland than anywhere else – especially by women. The game callers have their own bingo 'lingo' with names for the numbers, like 'two little ducks' for 22, so it's a real experience attending a game. It was introduced by the Catholic Church, who used the profits for the upkeep of the church building. Bingo evenings take place in the community halls or at the *National Stadium. Tue, Thu and Sun | South Circular Road | tel. 01 4 53 33 71 or 01 4 54 35 25)*

## CINEMA

### INSIDER TIP IRISH FILM INSTITUTE ●
(108 C4) (ℳ F5)

If you are looking for a sophisticated art house film, you should head for the Irish Film Institute (IFI). The institute shows classics, short and documentary films as well as new independent Irish releases. It also hosts an annual international film festival. If you need a break during the day in Temple Bar, the INSIDER TIP IFI Café is an ideal place for a simple meal at reasonable prices. Alongside is a well stocked film bookshop. *6 Eustace Street | tel. 01 6 79 34 77 | www.irishfilm.ie | bus: Temple Bar*

### SCREEN
(109 D3) (ℳ G5)

This cinema theatre, a favourite among the youth, has three cinemas (two of which have double seats for couples) and shows mainstream blockbusters as well as some more sophisticated independent films. Take a look at the beautiful INSIDER TIP bronze statue of an usher in front of the cinema. *D'Olier Street | tel. 01 6 72 55 00 | bus: College Green*

## LIVE MUSIC

### THE BRAZEN HEAD ★ ●
(108 A4) (ℳ F5)

Officially Ireland's oldest pub, The Brazen Head was apparently founded in 1198. Its medieval crenellated façade is lit with flaming torches and welcomes guests in true pub style. While the year of origin may be doubtful, it is true that there has been a tavern here since 1600. Every evening there is live traditional music in the packed hall next to the paved courtyard *20 Lower Bridge Street | tel. 01 6 77 95 49 | www.brazenhead.com | free admission | Luas: Four Courts*

### THE COBBLESTONE ★
(112 B6) (ℳ E4)

The décor may leave much to be desired but good music is the real attraction here. A sign in the musicians' area next to the entrance says, 'Listening area – please respect musicians' so talking during the music session is frowned upon. In the pub itself the atmosphere is more relaxed and music is played in INSIDER TIP *The Backroom* on the lower floor where new and established bands perform for large audiences. This place has an authentic Irish atmosphere, which connoisseurs of the Irish music scene will appreciate. *77 North King St. | tel. 01 8 72 17 99 | Luas: Smithfield*

**MARCO POLO HIGHLIGHTS**

**CRAWDADDY** ⭐ (114 C3) (*ɯ G6*)
Not a massive club but Crawdaddy is big on quality and caters to an audience with taste so they like to bring in new as well as well known musicians from the around the world. African rhythms, jazz and reggae are often part of the programme. The connecting *Lobby Bar* is the perfect place to have a drink before the concert. Friday is club night and under the name *515@ Crawdaddy,* house, hip-hop and more are played well into the night. *Opening times depend on event | Harcourt St. | tel. 01 6 22 43 05 | www.pod.ie | Luas: Harcourt*

**O'DONOGHUE'S** (109 E6) (*ɯ G5*)
This simple pub enjoys a legendary reputation due to the quality of the Irish music that you can hear here every evening. O'Donoghue's is best known as the birthplace of the band *The Dubliners*. Neither the fame of the pub nor the tourists that pop in here constantly have impacted on its cosy atmosphere. On warmer days the guests like to drink their Guinness at the standing tables outside. *15 Merrion Row | tel. 01 6 60 71 94 | www.odonoghuesbar. com | Luas: St Stephen's Green*

**HUGHES' BAR** ● (108 A3) (*ɯ F5*)
A rather large pub that is not very atmospheric but what it lacks in atmosphere it makes up for with its excellent traditional Irish music sessions – one of the best Dublin has to offer. *20 Chancery St. | www. dublinpubscene.com/thepubs/mhughes | Luas: Four Courts*

**SWEENEY'S MONGREL** (108 C4) (*ɯ G5*)
Bar with live music every night – from reggae to jazz to traditional Irish music. If you prefer a quiet evening you can retreat to other parts of the pub: the establishment extends over three floors. *32 Dame Street | tel. 01 4 17 00 00 | www. dublinsessions.ie/sweeneys.html | bus: Dame Street*

**TEMPLE BAR MUSIC CENTRE**
(108 C4) (*ɯ F5*)
Primary focus here is new, innovative musicians and bands – but well known artists like Van Morrison have also performed here. *Curved St. | tel. 01 6 70 92 02 | www. tbmc.ie | bus: Temple Bar*

**VICAR STREET** (114 B2) (*ɯ F5*)
This establishment has twice been voted Ireland's best music venue. The performances go across the entire music spectrum from folk and traditional music to black country, pop, blues and jazz. *8 Thomas St. | www.vicarstreet.com | bus: Thomas St.*

**INSIDER TIP** **WHELAN'S** (114 C3) (*ɯ F6*)
A simple traditional pub that is also a very famous music venue that caters to all

---

# LOW BUDGET

▶ The beer on the outskirts of the city may be cheaper, but in many pubs in the city centre there is also ● live music – without having to pay an admission fee. Good options: *The Brazen Head (Bridge Street), Oliver St John Gogarty (Fleet Street)* and especially *Hughes' Bar,* where you can also often hear the bagpipes being playing *(19 Chancery St. | Luas: Four Courts).*

▶ In July and August there is an r open-air cinema every Saturday from 9.30pm at the *Meeting House Square* in Temple Bar. They show mostly classics and admission is free. Tickets: *Temple Bar Information Centre | 12 East Essex Street | www.visit-templebar.ie*

Mulligan's: no better place in Dublin for a pint of perfectly poured draft Guinness

sorts: rock, indie, traditional, electronic and Irish. The Wexford Street is the epicentre of the slightly rundown *Village Quarter* area. Other music venues nearby are *The Village (26 Wexford St.)* and *Anseo (28 Camden St.)*. *25 Wexford St. | tel. 01 478 07 66 | www.whelanslive.com | Luas: St Stephen's Green*

## PUBS

### FOGGY DEW (108 C4) (*ω G5*)
Small historic pub on the outskirts of Temple Bar. In the afternoon you can enjoy a leisurely pint, in the evenings it gets a bit louder and wilder: disco music and Sundays live concerts. *1 Fownes St. Upper | www.thefoggydew.ie | bus: Dame Street*

### INTERNATIONAL BAR (109 D4) (*ω G5*)
The third generation family that runs this pub wants to keep its authentic Irish character and doesn't exploit its mention in James Joyce's novel 'Ulysses'. The price of the Guinness here is also relatively palatable and the audience is a pleasant mix of young and old, chic and shabby. The basement and rooms above are also popular comedy and jazz venues. *Wicklow St. | bus: Dame St.*

### MULLIGAN'S ★ ● (109 E3) (*ω G5*)
If you have a look around in this old pub, you will know why it has been an institute in Dublin for generations. Dark wood, discrete nooks and theatre posters create an atmosphere that even James Joyce and John F. Kennedy (as a young newspaper reporter) could treasure. And no one pours Guinness better than the crew behind this counter. *8 Poolbeg St. | DART: Tara St.*

### INSIDER TIP ▶ THE LONG HALL (114 C2) (*ω F5*)
Wonderfully authentic pub where ordinary Dubliners like to meet up for a drink. The room is long and narrow with lots of mirrored glass, crystal chandeliers and carved wood. *51 South Great George's St. | bus: South Great George's St.*

### THE PORTERHOUSE (108 B4) (*F5*)

This popular pub with bar counters on several floors is a stroke of luck for beer lovers. No one in Dublin has a negative word to say about Guinness, because here the black elixir of life is beyond reproach. However, this also means that Dublin has a kind of beer monoculture as the draft beer on tap in every pub is Guinness and their affiliated beer brands. The **INSIDER TIP ▶** ing attracts a young crowd, which prefers a traditional pub to the trendy contemporary style of many of the new places. Hot meals are available until the early evening and later on the room pulsates with music from the DJ *(Fri–Sun)* or live bands *(Mon–Thu)*. The selection of international beers is far larger than in most other pubs. *14–15 Ormond Quay | between Chapel St. and Arran St. East | Luas: Jervis*

At Stag's Head it is not about hunting trophies, but the rather wonderful Victorian interior

micro brewery *Porterhouse* on the other hand, brews their own excellent quality beer. Try *Porterhouse Red, Plain Oyster Stout* or their *Templebräu* pilsner which is brewed with German hops. Classic pub fare of bangers and mash or Irish stew. At weekends there is live music. *16–18 Parliament St. | bus: Temple Bar*

### SIN E (108 B3) (*F5*)

This simply furnished, long narrow establishment with low ceilings and dim light-

### THE STAG'S HEAD ★
(108 C4) (*G5*)

The interior of this Victorian pub is well worth seeing: stained glass windows, a mounted 'Stag's Head', red plush seats, dark wood, old mirrors and marble topped tables. At weekends this pub, hidden in a small alleyway between Trinity Street and South Great George's Street, is packed and there is live music in the basement and an additional bar on the first floor. *1 Dame Court | bus: Dame St.*

## DANCE

### COISCEIM

This creative modern dance ensemble (the name means 'footsteps') under the leading Irish choreographer David Bolger is a sensation both at home and internationally. Performances take place at various venues, often at *Project Arts Centre (39 Essex St. East | tickets 10am–6pm | tel. 01 8 81 96 13 | www.project.ie | bus: Temple Bar). Info at tel. 01 8 78 05 58 | www.coisceim.com*

### O'SHEA'S MERCHANT

(108 A4) (*ⵎ F5*)

Traditional Irish set dancing has a stronger following in the provinces than in Dublin, where the younger audience prefers international and modern dancing. However, the large pub O'Shea still likes to maintain tradition and there is a section in the back where traditional music sessions take place. The pub serves suitably hearty meals like Irish stew. *12 Bridge St. Lower | music and dance every night | free admission | Luas: Four Courts*

## THEATRE & SHOWS

### ABBEY THEATRE

(109 D2) (*ⵎ G4*)

Since its foundation in 1904 the Abbey Theatre has a prominent place in the cultural life of this literature-obsessed country. The stage encouraged a generation of Irish to produce a body of literary work now known as the Irish Literary Revival, to whom Ireland's first Nobel laureate, William Butler Yeats also belonged. Riots broke out during the premiere performance of the 'shocking' new work, Sean O'Casey's 'The Plough and the Stars', because the public felt that the left-wing dramatist had not treated Ireland's rebel history with enough respect. In 1951 the song 'Keep the Home Fires Burning' played at the closing of the performance, then the theatre burned down and it was only in 1966 that it was rebuilt. At the reopening 'The Plough and the Stars' was once again performed but this time around there was no scandal. Today the Abbey is well known for its excellent productions. The smaller studio stage *The Peacock* dedicates itself mostly to the works of new dramatists. *26 Abbey Street Lower | tickets Mon–Sat 10.30am–7pm | tel. 01 8 78 72 22 | www.abbeytheatre.ie | Luas: Abbey Street*

### GAIETY THEATRE

(109 D5) (*ⵎ G5*)

The extravagant design of this 1871 theatre is in itself worth the visit. The productions are suitable for a wide audience: musicals, famous dramas, concerts and operas. *King Street South | tickets Mon–Sat 10am–6pm | tel. 01 6 77 17 17 | www.gaietytheatre.com | Luas: St Stephen's Green*

### GATE THEATRE ★

(112 C5) (*ⵎ G4*)

A wonderful 18th century theatre makes an excellent backdrop for performances of works by well known European and American authors, but also young Irish talents. The Gate is also an important venue for Samuel Beckett fans. *1 Cavendish Row (at Parnell Square) | tickets Mon–Sat 10am until 7.30pm | tel. 01 8 74 40 45 | www.gate-theatre.ie | bus: O'Connell St.*

### GRAND CANAL THEATRE

(115 E1) (*ⵎ H5*)

The theatre in the Docklands was designed by star architect Daniel Libeskind. It produces ballets, musicals, classic orchestra music and opera. *Grand Canal Square | tel. (*) 08 18 71 93 77 | www.grandcanaltheatre.ie | Dart: Pearse Street/Grand Canal Dock*

# WHERE TO STAY

**Irish hospitality is legendary, and while it is more evident in the rural countryside, it is happily also alive and well in Irish cities.**

Luxurious hostels, relaxed family hotels, exclusive boutique hotels or private accommodation in bed and breakfasts – they all offer their guests a heartfelt welcome. Dublin is a financial centre as well as a popular tourist destination and the city caters to both those on business trips and tourists. Due to the Irish financial crisis hotel prices have dropped somewhat but it is also worth negotiating a discount – especially if you want to book for several nights. However, during the peak season, or over big sporting events or city conventions, hotel rates are not negotiable and there are no discounts.

Generally the overnight room price also includes a very filling cooked Irish breakfast, or at the very least, a continental breakfast. It is worth confirming this when making your booking as some of the luxury hotels charge separately for breakfast.

If the focus of your Dublin visit is more about the nightlife, then you should stay in the centre of town. But if you are looking for a more natural outdoor environment and fresh air to relax in after a sightseeing (or shopping) tour in Dublin, then a better

Photo: Discreet luxury in the Shelbourne Hotel

**Dublin may never sleep but you will certainly need to ... and some comfortable accommodation is always welcome**

bet for you would be the suburbs on the coast or at Phoenix Park, where there are a number of suitable options.

The city's magnificent Georgian architecture remains one of Dublin's main attractions and it goes without saying that you shouldn't only enjoy it from the outside – you should book into a hotel in one of the city's fine 18th century townhouses. If money is not an issue, then the *Merrion Hotel* should be your first choice while *Staunton's on the Green* and *Harrington Hall* will be a little easier on your pocket.

Finally there are also a large number of shared rooms in privately run youth and backpacker hostels, as Dublin is a magnet for young tourists from all over the world. The official tourist information *Dublin Tourism* offers an excellent accommodation

Guests at the Shelbourne enjoying the splendour of a bygone era

service including online bookings at *www.visitdublin.com.* Keep an eye out for specials and last-minute deals. Advice and bookings are also possible telephonically or directly at the offices of *Dublin Tourism* at the airport and in the city centre. The website *www.dublinks.com* is also a good source.

## HOTELS: EXPENSIVE

### DEER PARK HOTEL HOWTH
(117 F4) (*Ø O*)
The best aspect of this hotel, a rather unspectacular building from the 1970s, is its position in the grounds of the large estate of *Howth Castle,* with its golf course and its famous Rhododendron Gardens – the **INSIDER TIP** flowering period at end of May is the best time to stay here.
There are rooms with sea views, a swimming pool, tennis courts and wellness centre, as well as the *Four Earls Restaurant* which the guests can also make use of. Howth, with its harbour and local seafood restaurants, is a comfortable walk away. Take a walk up ● ⅍ *Howth Heath* behind the hotel and you will be rewarded with a lovely view over the town and the bay. *84 rooms | Deer Park | Howth | tel. 01 8 32 34 89 | www.deerpark-hotel.ie | DART: Howth*

### FITZPATRICK CASTLE HOTEL
(117 F5) (*Ø O*)
This spectacular 18th century hotel is home to an award-winning restaurant as well as an extensive fitness area. Due to its favourable location, you can be at the beach or in the hills of Killiney in only a few minutes, and to get to Dublin city centre it will only take you 20 minutes on the DART. *113 rooms | Killiney Hill Road | Killiney | tel. 01 2 30 54 00 | www.fitzpatrick castle.com | DART: Dalkey*

### GRESHAM HOTEL (109 D1) (*Ø G4*)
The Gresham has been accommodating sophisticated visitors since 1817. In the recent past the ravages of time were tak-

ing their toll on the 'old lady', but a recent renovation has made sure that its impressive façade and the large lobby live up to their promise. If you cannot afford to stay overnight, but still want to enjoy its elegant style, then drop in for a delicious afternoon tea between 2pm and 6pm. *289 rooms | 23 O'Connell St. Upper | tel. 01 8 74 68 81 | www.gresham-hotels.com | airport bus: 747, 748, Aircoach O'Connell St.*

### NUMBER 31 (115 D3) (*⊡ G6*)
Run by a married couple, the Comers, this Georgian house on Fitzwilliam Place (and a modern extension on Leeson Close) lies in one of the most elegant suburbs of Dublin. All rooms en suite and are individually decorated, breakfast is served in a wonderful conservatory, and they always give their guest a warm and friendly reception. Parking is available. *21 rooms | 31 Leeson Close | tel. 01 6 76 50 11 | www.number31.ie | bus: Aircoach Leeson St. Lower*

### THE SHELBOURNE (109 D6) (*⊡ G5*)
A true Dublin institute. The heritage rooms in the old wing maintain the elegance of a bygone era. A little less expensive, but still very luxurious, are the rooms in the modern wing. Afternoon tea in the *Lord Mayor's Lounge* is a real experience and you will find celebrities at the ● *Horseshoe Bar*, while in the INSIDERTIP ▶ *Oyster Bar* high society meets to eat oysters and drink champagne. *265 rooms | 27 St Stephen's Green | tel. 01 6 63 45 00 | www.marriott. com | Aircoach: St Stephen's Green*

## HOTELS: MODERATE

### ARIEL HOUSE ★ (115 F3) (*⊡ J6*)
This hotel is in the quiet and pretty suburb of Ballsbridge, south-east of the city centre. It is in a stylish 19th century house and has been furnished with an eye for

detail and is full of antiques. All rooms have their own bathrooms and the city centre is within easy walking distance. *37 rooms | 50–54 Lansdowne Road | tel. 01 6 68 55 12 | www.ariel-house.net | DART: Lansdowne Road*

### BUSWELL'S HOTEL (109 E5) (*⊡ G5*)
Buswell's Hotel may not be very fashionable but its location – in the middle of the city and near all the best shopping areas – makes it a good choice. The Georgian architecture of its three historic townhouses is matched by its classic dark wooden furniture and décor. Guests can use the secure parking and eat and drink in the comfortable *Buswell's Bar*. *67 rooms | 23–27 Molesworth St. | tel. 01 6 14 65 00 | www.buswells.ie | bus: Aircoach Merrion Square*

### THE CENTRAL (108 C4) (*⊡ F5*)
Established in 1887, this is one of the oldest hotels in Dublin. The rooms are very

---

**MARCO POLO HIGHLIGHTS**

★ **Ariel House**
Stylish hotel in a leafy suburb
→ p. 81

★ **Harrington Hall**
Welcoming Georgian hotel that was once a hostel run by nuns → p. 82

★ **Clarence Hotel**
Just the way U2 like it: luxury and style directly on the river
→ p. 82

★ **Trinity College**
Live where others study: rooms in the 400-year-old university
→ p. 84

modern and offer everything that you can expect from a 3-star hotel. In its *Library Bar* with all its old books, time seems to have come to a stand still. *70 rooms | 1–5 Exchequer St. | tel. 01 6 79 73 02 | www.centralhoteldublin.com | bus: Dame Street/ South Great George's Street*

### HARRINGTON HALL ⭐
(114 C3) *(ᴍ G6)*

Only a few hotels in the city centre have the personal touch offered by this family business near St Stephen's Green. After extensive renovations – in beautiful blue and yellow tones – the Georgian house now offers far more comfort than it did in days gone by when it was a young women's hostel run by nuns. Free parking and a good breakfast are also available. Ask for a ▶INSIDER TIP◀ room on the first floor – the windows are larger and the view on to the streets better. *28 rooms | 70 Harcourt St. | tel. 01 4 75 34 97 | www.harringtonhall.com | Luas: Harcourt*

# LUXURY HOTELS

### Clarence Hotel ⭐ (108 C3) *(ᴍ G5)*

U2 musician Bono and Edge liked this venerable old hotel in the Temple Bar so much that they bought it and re-developed it into a chic boutique hotel. The rooms are individually furnished and have bathrooms that are the epitome of quality and luxury. Double rooms from 220 euro, with a view onto the Liffey over 300 euro. *49 rooms | 6–8 Wellington Quay | tel. 01 4 07 08 00 | www.theclarence.ie | bus: Temple Bar*

### Dylan Hotel (115 E3) *(ᴍ H6)*

Behind the richly decorated brick façade of this former nurses' home is a designer hotel with individually furnished rooms (from 200 euro) in an exuberant style. It is located in a leafy residential area south of Grand Canal and not far from the city centre. *44 rooms | Eastmoreland Place | tel. 01 6 60 30 00 | www.dylan.ie | Aircoach: Northumberland Rd., then a walk*

### Merrion Hotel (109 E6) *(ᴍ G5)*

State guests like to stay in this complex of buildings comprising of four elegant 18th century townhouses conveniently situated just across from the Irish Parliament. The Duke of Wellington was born in no. 24. The interior design is a blend of classical (no. 22) and rococo (no. 21). There is a swimming pool, wellness area and two restaurants, one of which is the Michelin star and award-winning *Restaurant Patrick Guilbaud*. Double rooms from 410 euro. *142 rooms | Upper Merrion Street | tel. 01 6 03 06 00 | www.merrionhotelcom | bus: Aircoach Merrion Square*

### Morrison Hotel (108 C3) *(ᴍ F5)*

The fashion designer John Rocha is responsible for the design of this ultra-cool hotel. Located on the north bank of the Liffey, its Georgian façade hides a stylish and hip interior design, which contrasts soft tones with bolder ochre, red and gold tones. The rooms are furnished with artworks and first-class sound systems. The Japanese style *Lobo* nightclub and the restaurant *Halo* are in the same building. Double rooms from 175 euro. *138 rooms | Ormond Quay | tel. 01 8 74 40 39 | www.morrison hotelie | Luas: Jervis*

## JURY'S INN CUSTOM HOUSE
**(109 F3)** *(∅ G4)*

The 3-star hotel in the Docklands, near the Custom House, belongs to a chain known for its reliable quality. In case this category is right, but you don't like the location – the areas opposite Christ Church Cathedral and in Parnell Street have some more Jury's Inns. *239 rooms | Custom House Quay | tel. 01 6 07 50 00 | www. jurysinns.com | DART/Luas: Connolly*

## KELLY'S HOTEL
**(108 C5)** *(∅ F5)*

The hotel above *Hogan's Bar* is sparsely furnished but nonetheless offers everything you need and the French cuisine hotel restaurant, *L'Gueuleton,* is considered to be one of the best places to eat out in Dublin. And its *Secret Bar* is famous for its mojitos. *16 rooms | 36 South Great George's St. | tel. 01 6 48 00 10 | www.kellysdublin. com | bus: South Great George's Street*

## TEMPLE BAR HOTEL
**(109 D3)** *(∅ G5)*

A modern hotel in the centre of the city's entertainment district, which means that it can get rather loud. The 129 rooms have modern furnishings and Internet is free. Look out for their special offers, e.g. three nights for the price of two. Its bright conservatory-style *Terrace Restaurant* is decorated with contemporary art. *Fleet Street | tel. 01 6 77 33 33 | www.templebar hotel.com | bus: Fleet Street/Westmore-land Street*

## THE TOWNHOUSE **(109 E2)** *(∅ G4)*

The hotel, run by very friendly staff, consists of two old townhouses with modern extensions. The beds are comfortable, the rooms well furnished, and the breakfasts are generous. O'Connell Street is five minutes away on foot and the bus stop for the airport buses is just down the road. *40 rooms | 47–48 Lower Gardiner St. | tel.*

A man of the world: the doorman at the Merrion Hotel

*01 8 78 88 08 | www.townhouseofdublin. com | Luas: Busáras , airport bus 747, 748*

## HOTELS: BUDGET

**INSIDER TIP** ABC GUESTHOUSE
**(113 D2)** *(∅ G2)*

A friendly reception, a generous breakfast and three clean rooms (in varying sizes) await visitors to this reasonably priced bed and breakfast in the north of Dublin. It is right on the bus route between the airport and inner city. *57 Drumcondra Road Upper | tel. 01 8 36 74 17 | www.abchouse dublin.com | bus from airport: 16A, 41, 746 until the Skylon Hotel stop; from inner city plenty of bus routes, e.g. 3, 16, 41*

## HOTEL ISAACS **(109 E2)** *(∅ G4)*

This hotel, centrally located at the bus station, is in a converted wine warehouse. There are even a few rooms especially for smokers. The hotel restaurant, *Il Vignardo,* offers you an extended Happy Hour with rather good prices. You can **INSIDER TIP** book the airport bus at half price on the website. Lodging in a shared room from 18 euro, double room from 74 euro. *103 rooms | Store Street | tel. 01 8 13 47 00 | www.isaacs.ie | bus: Busáras, DART/Luas: Connolly Station*

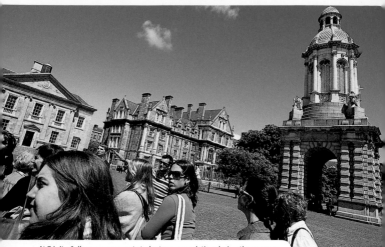

At Trinity College you can rent student accommodation during the summer

### PHOENIX PARK HOUSE 111 F5) *(💧 E4)*

Their single, double and family rooms are all en suite and tastefully furnished, and their excellent breakfast is also available as a vegetarian option. For joggers, and everyone who enjoys a breath of fresh air in the big city, Phoenix Park is right on the doorstep, also conveniently situated near Heuston Station. *29 rooms | 38–39 Parkgate St. | tel. 01 6 77 28 70 | www.dublinguesthouse.com | airport bus 748 and Luas: Heuston*

## HOSTELS & STUDENT ACCOMMODATION

### AVALON HOUSE (108 C6) *(💧 F5)*

Single, double, four bed and shared rooms from 15 euro incl. breakfast are on offer. The hostel is in a characterful building that was once a medical school. Temple Bar and St Stephen's Green are both within walking distance. Kitchen, Internet and lockers are available. *281 beds | 55 Aungier Street | tel. 01 4 75 00 01 | www.avalon-house.ie | bus: 16A from airport*

### INSIDER TIP GLOBETROTTERS
(109 E2) *(💧 G4)*

This backpacker hostel has clean rooms with six, eight, ten or twelve beds in the basement and the back rooms of an historic townhouse. It is somewhat quieter than others, which are situated closer to Temple Bar. And it has the added advantage of having a generous Irish breakfast included in the price. There is also free Internet usage and guests have the use of the courtyard garden. *60 beds | 46–48 Lower Gardiner Street | tel. 01 8 73 58 93 | www.globetrottersdublin.com | airport buses 41 and 41C stop in front of the door, Luas: Busáras*

### TRINITY COLLEGE ★
(109 D4) *(💧 G5)*

During the semester holidays, from June to September, the university rents out historic and modern student rooms to tourists. The accommodation is quite acceptable and the characters of the rooms vary. Many have a beautiful view on to the old courtyards of the college and about half of them have their own bathrooms. There are also double rooms and small apartments with kitchens. Bed and breakfast 60 euro/person. *800 rooms | Trinity College | tel. 01 6 08 11 77 | www. tcd.ie/accommodation/Visitors | bus: Aircoach Grafton St.*

## APARTMENTS

### IVY EXCHANGE APARTMENTS
(108 C4) (*ш F4*)

These apartments are situated near O'Connell Street which means that you can reach most of the places of interest, the shopping areas and the entertainment district Temple Bar, quite comfortably on foot. In Parnell Street there are a number of cheap Asian restaurants. Opposite is Moore Street with its vegetable sellers as well as countless new African and Asian shops. The apartments accommodate 4 people and consist of two bedrooms, open plan kitchen, living room and bathroom. The prices start at 70 euro per apartment per night. If you book 14 days ahead and pay the full amount, you receive a discount. When booking, you should indicate whether you would like to have a parking space in the underground parking lot *(12 euro/ 24 hrs)*, which is advisable as parking in the city centre is limited. *166–168 Parnell Street | Parnell Square | tel. 01 6 77 66 00 | book at www.staydublin.com | bus: Parnell Square*

### OLIVER ST. JOHN GOGARTY
### PENTHOUSE APARTMENTS ✵
(109 D3) (*ш G5*)

These apartments are on the fifth floor above the famous pub *Oliver St John Gogarty* and are in the middle of the Temple Bar entertainment district. Despite their location they are very quiet and a great alternative to an expensive hotel

in the city centre for a INSIDER TIP family vacation.

Five of the apartments have two bedrooms that sleep a maximum of four persons, a further apartment offers three bedrooms for six people, and all contain a living and dining room as well as kitchen. The view over the roofs of Dublin is astounding, the central location unbeatable and the price *(apartment for 4 Mon–Fri 99, Sat/Sun 150–175 euro/night; apartment for 6 Mon– Fri 129, Sat/Sun 200 euro/night)* very reasonable. *6 apts. | 18–21 Anglesea St. | tel. 01 6 711 8 22 | www.olivergogartys.com | bus: Aircoach Grafton St.*

## LOW BUDGET

▶ If you want to be able to party and then fall straight into bed, the best place for you is the backpacker hostel *Barnacles* in the middle of the bustling Temple Bar district. The hostel is clean and safe and its rooms are light and quite spacious. Double rooms available from 30 euro, in the communal rooms you pay as little as 10 euro a night. *1 Cecilia St. | tel. 01 6 716 2 77 | www.barnacles.ie*

▶ *Mercer Court* is a student residence that rents out 100 en suite rooms to Dublin visitors during the student holidays between the end of June and September. They are cheaper than Trinity College and are often of a better standard. Centrally located near St Stephen's Green, single rooms from 60 euro, double rooms from 90 euro. Booking at *www.visitdublin. com* see under 'campus accommodation'. *Lower Mercer Street | tel. 01 4 78 03 28 | Luas: St Stephen's Green*

# WALKING TOURS

The tours are marked in green in the street atlas, the pull-out map and on the back cover

## 1 IN THE FOOTSTEPS OF IRISH FREEDOM FIGHTERS

Ireland's independence is not a topic that can be overlooked in Dublin. From the nationalists' perspective, the issue of an independent Irish state was only partly resolved in 1921 because six counties in Northern Ireland are still part of the United Kingdom. There are numerous museums and monuments throughout the city that commemorate the events of the Easter Rising 1916 (and other important dates) and this 1.5 hour walk guides you through Ireland's road to independence.

In the middle of the street on College Green is a statue of Henry Grattan who successfully campaigned for the independence of the Irish Parliament from the London government in 1782. With an upraised right arm he looks out on to Trinity College, the training grounds for the Protestant regime that ruled over the Catholic majority in Ireland. Today the parliament building left of Grattan houses the Bank of Ireland → p. 35. The legislative independence survived less than 20 years. The rebellion of 1798 followed the renewed incorporation of the Irish back under British parliamentary control. Cross over College Green towards the bank then

Photo: Custom House on the Liffey's north bank

Follow Ireland's steps to independence and also take a stroll around some of the neighbourhoods where ordinary Dubliners live

turn right and go around the building, at the traffic lights cross Westmoreland Street to the statue of Thomas Moore (1779–1852), who the Irish celebrate as their national poet, and then go left on to O'Connell Bridge. On the north side of the bridge is the impressive O'Connell Monument. Daniel O'Connell (1775–1847), whom the Irish see as their liberator and 'uncrowned king', instigated the Catholic Emancipation. In 1841 he became the first Catholic mayor of Dublin. The four winged female figures around his statue represent Ireland's provinces. One of them has a bullet hole in the chest from the 1916 Easter Rising.

Stay north of the Liffey and take the walkway on the right next to the river to the next bridge, Butt Bridge. Cross over the Liffey, go to the right across the street and you have a wonderful view behind the railway bridge of the **Custom House's** → p. 42 façade. In 1921 the section of the building that housed the British administration burned down. The damage is evidenced by the newer tower's brown colour which is where cheaper stone was used for the reconstruction.

Go back under the railway bridge, cross over the riverbank street and continue a few steps to the **statue of James Connolly**. The labour leader looks out on to the trade union centre **Liberty Hall**. The plough and stars behind him symbolise work and socialism. Connolly was a commander of the 1916 Easter Rising, and he was seriously injured during the occupation of the General Post Office (GPO). He was executed in Kilmainham Gaol – chained to a chair, because he was unable stand in front of the firing squad.

Cross over Beresford Place to Abbey Street and to the **Abbey Theatre** → p. 77. Across the road three bronze heads on small pillars demarcate the place where the Irish national flag was unveiled for the first time in 1848. IThe tricolour flag has green for Ireland, orange for the royalist Protestant Orange and white for the hope that the two will reconcile.

Turn right into O'Connell Street and you will soon be standing in front of the **General Post Office** → p. 44, the rebels' headquarters in 1916. On Easter Monday a small group barricaded themselves in the GPO and stayed there for four days under artillery fire. The building became a burning ruin and the survivors fled along Henry Street (turning left from the GPO) and along Moore Street (on the right). The lane right of the northern end of Moore Street, shortly before the spot where the rebels capitulated, is called **O'Rahilly Parade**. On the wall INSIDER TIP a plaque commemorates the rebel *Michael O'Rahilly* and has the words of the last letter that the fatally wounded man wrote to his wife saying: 'It was a good fight anyhow. Goodbye, darling'. The 1916 rising was insignificant in a military sense, but the severe retaliatory measures turned the rebels into martyrs, the GPO into the nation's shrine and the fight for independence into a movement with broad support from the population.

## 2 TRADERS, SAINTS AND VIKINGS

**Over centuries Dublin's city centre moved further and further east. The 2.5 hour walk to the capital's beginnings leads through the Liberties, where life takes on a different pace than in the chic city centre, and ends at the former trader's area and current entertainment district of Temple Bar.**

The tour begins at **St Patrick's Park**, where the lawns and flower beds make a pretty frame for the view of the **Cathedral** → p. 41. A fountain on the south-west corner of the park is apparently where St Patrick converted and baptised people into Christianity in the 5th century. The cathedral was built on an island on the river Poddle (today it is an underground river), whose dark waters formed a 'black lake', in Gaelic *Dubh Linn*, and which gave the city its name. Take a look inside the cathedral before crossing Patrick Street and Hanover Lane to reach **Francis Street** with is antique dealers. Here you will find interesting shops with ceramics, clocks and much more, the route then continues to the right in a northerly direction. You will see the **Church of St Nicholas**, completed in 1832, which was only allowed once the anti-Catholic laws were abolished in 1829. Further along you will see the ornate brick work of the **Iveagh Market**, built in 1907, which is waiting to be restored and repurposed. Across the road lies the **Tivoli Theatre** and on the corner of Cornmarket you can relax with a good coffee at **Caffé Noto**.

This district, the **Liberties → p. 48**, is currently undergoing a change. The small shops on Thomas Street and Meath Street are for people with a more modest income. Students from the nearby College of Art and Design lend a creative flair to

left and you will see **INSIDER TIP** *Taylor's Hall* a charming brick building dating back to 1706. The tailors' guild house is a rare remnant from the time when this was a district of artisans and traders.

Cross over the traffic lights at the junction of **St Audoen Church → p. 41** on the northern side of High Street. The streets Cornmarket and High Street eastward to Dame

Green lawns and trees frame the Gothic cathedral: St Patrick's Park

the district, and the influence of immigrants from Eastern Europe is also noticeable. Take a detour to the left, to the fake rock grotto behind the **St Catherine's Church → p. 48** on Meath Street and to the colourful and over the top interior of the **Augustinian Church** on **Thomas Street → p. 48** and you will see how popular religious piety is expressed.

At Cornmarket the route goes towards the east. Go right at the corner to Lamb Alley and you will see a remnant of the original medieval city wall. In the next lane on the right, **Back Lane**, go about 100m to the

Street demarcate the hill where the Vikings founded a trading settlement in the 10th century. The elevation becomes clear when you take the road between St Audouen and the park on the western side. Between the high stone walls it leads down to **St Audoen's Gate**, the city gate that dates back to 1275, and the original section of the preserved city wall. Follow Cook Street to the right and cross Winetavern Street. The **City Council Civic Office** administrative building is now in the place of the former Viking settlement. In the area in front of the building archaeologists found various items from Viking daily life – household goods, tools, combs and coins, which are now on display at the *National Museum*. Essex Street leads you further to the lanes and alleys of Temple Bar → p. 34 once a neighbourhood of merchants and traders.

## ③ A TASTE OF DUBLIN'S EVERYDAY LIFE

This one hour walk takes you off the beaten track and shows you the parts of the city that tourists don't usually get to see: a normal shopping street, the wholesale market, the law courts and the parish churches. The morning is the best time for this tour.

Temple Bar, Dublin's entertainment district

The route starts in Capel Street north of the Liffey *(Luas: Jervis)*. The street offers a wonderful variety of shops: there are shops for new clothes and vintage fashion, a computer store and pet store, making it an eclectic mix of chic and shabby. There are Irish traders with mobile fruit stalls and Polish and Korean vendors selling groceries which their people would usually not find in Ireland. Leave Capel Street between the Liffey and Parnell Street and cross Little Mary Street to the wholesale market which has Corinthian columns marking the entrance of the beautiful old market hall. Take care around here because there are some wild forklift drivers! Take a leisurely walk through the stalls selling fruit, vegetables and flowers. On the other side of the market hall it is only a few steps to the Four Courts → p. 44, where lawyers in robes rush to their trials and the nervous participants grab a quick cigarette before their hearing. This is also where some important and sensational trials take place and even though the criminal court moved to a new building near Phoenix Park in 2010, the striking dome of the Four Courts still frequently appears in the television news.

If you would like to do some more sightseeing, walk further west to St Michan's Church → p. 47 or to the Jameson Distillery → p. 45. But this tour now turns to the left behind the Four Courts into Church Street and crosses over Liffey via the Father Matthew Bridge. The father whom the bridge is named after preached abstinence in the 19th century. If you would like to learn more about his teachings, go past Dublin's oldest pub The Brazen Head → p. 73 south of the bridge and turn from Bridge Street right into Wormwood Gate. From there turn left then right and left again into John Street and to the beautiful *St Augustine's Church* on Thomas Street, where the walk ends.

Here – within sniffing distance from the Guinness Brewery – you are in the Liberties → p. 48, Dublin's oldest district. If you still have the energy, you can walk on to the Guinness Storehouse → p. 49 or cross Francis Street to St Patrick's Cathedral → p. 41. There are a number of different buses that will take you back to the city centre.

## 4 GLASNEVIN CEMETERY, IRELAND'S NECROPOLIS

More than 1.2 million people have been laid to rest in Ireland's national cemetery – more than Dublin's inhabitants – and all its important citizens are buried here. A walk through the cemetery is a walk through Dublin's troubled history. *Daily 9am–6pm | bus: Finglas Road/Glasnevin Cemetery*

Start your tour at Finglas Road where you will find the main entrance to the old cemetery. Also here is the Museum → p. 49 which is well worth a visit *(Mon–Fri 10am–5pm, Sat–Sun 11am–5pm | admission fee 6 euro | www.glasnevinmuseum.ie)*. On the right behind the building, at the cemetery wall, is where Michael Collins is buried. He led the guerrilla war against the British occupiers and later went on to become Ireland's first Minister of Finance. He was killed in the 1922 civil war. His fiancé, Kitty Kiernan, is also buried close to his grave. Many visitors ask for Julia Roberts' grave because she played the role of Kitty Kiernan in the film 'Michael Collins'.

Now return to the tower at the main entrance where you will find the mausoleum of Daniel O'Connell below the tower. Dublin's main thoroughfare was named after him and he is famed for his fight for the rights of Catholic citizens. He also founded the cemetery, in 1832, so that

non-Anglicans could also receive a decent burial. In his time the site covered about 8 acres, but today it stretches over 123 acres. If you walk around the tower in an anti-clockwise direction, you will come across countless graves of Irish rebels: Roger Casement, Kevin Barry, Cathal Brugha, O'Donovan Rossa, Maud Gonne MacBride, Frank Ryan and Countess Markievicz (the only female leader in the Easter Rising who avoided execution). North of the tower Eamon de Valera is buried, another leader of the Easter Rising, who later served terms as the head of government and then went on to become Ireland's president.

Continue further round the tower and turn to your right, past a small church. If you turn right and then left you will come to Charles Stewart Parnell's grave. He fought for Irish independence as a leader in the Irish Parliament. His grave is quite plain in comparison to O'Connell's. Parnell was first put to rest in a mass grave for the poor, but later the grave was marked with a large but simple memorial stone. In the row behind it you will find the resting place of John Stanislaus Joyce, father of the writer James Joyce.

Turn to your right, and then take the second path to your right again, and you will pass the memorial to men who fell in the Boer War. A little bit further, take the fork to your right, then left again. Here, in the oldest part of the cemetery, you will find some impressive graves of less famous Irish. Then shortly before the main entrance, the Prospect Gate, take a detour to the right where you will find the grave of the writer and dramatist Brendan Behan, who drank himself to death at 41 years of age. But that shouldn't stop you from leaving the cemetery through the Prospect Gate and entering Kavanagh's Pub → p. 49, which the locals call 'Gravediggers', to have a pint.

# TRAVEL WITH KIDS

The Irish may be fond of children but their capital is expensive for families and not ideal for children. The city centre has throngs of people, busy roads and dangerous traffic. Nevertheless Dublin does have a lot to offer children. Parks – like Merrion Square, St Stephen's Green and the large Phoenix Park – all have rolling lawns ideal for children to romp around on. And there is also a **INSIDER TIP** playground on the east side of St Stephen's Green. There are also the buskers and **INSIDER TIP** very funny and creative street artists performing on pavements at Temple Bar and in Grafton Street and there are a number of fun bus trips suitable for all age groups. Children under five can use public transport free of charge while family tickets make admission fees to various museums and events more affordable.

## ATTRACTIONS

### DUBLIN ZOO (111 E4) (ØD4)
The zoo, in the middle of Phoenix Park, has been one of Dublin's main attractions since 1830. Apart from the popular big animals – lions, tigers, elephants, giraffes, and gorillas – there are many more favourites. The zoo's management take pride in their attention to the animals' welfare. *Nov–Jan 9.30am–4pm, Feb 9.30am–5pm, March–Sept 9.30am–6pm, Oct 9.30am–5.30pm (the African savannah closes 1.5 hours earlier respectively) | family ticket 43.50 euro | Phoenix Park | www.dublinzoo.ie*

### DUBLINIA (108 A4) (ØF5)
Time travel back to the Viking era and to Dublin in the Middle Ages. You can take a trip on a Viking ship, try on some Norsemen clothing, view a Viking house and learn their runic alphabet. Displays take you back 700 years ago and you can experience the sounds and smells of Dublin in the Middle Ages. *April–Sept daily 10am–5pm, Oct–March daily 10am–4.30pm | adults 7.50, children 5 euro, family ticket 23 euro | St Michaels Hill, Christchurch Cathedral | www.dublinia.ie | bus: Lord Edward St.*

### INSIDER TIP NATIONAL LEPRECHAUN MUSEUM ● (108 C3) (ØF4)
The leprechaun is a fairytale creature – a tiny cobbler who knows where great treasures of gold are hidden. There are countless

**Dublin's parks, its lush surroundings and its nearby coastline all offer ample opportunities and space for children to play and to explore**

stories about leprechauns caught by humans so that they would tell them the secret hiding place. But because the leprechaun is sly and can do magic, they often have the upper hand. The museum is dedicated to this mythical Irish creature whose history is explained in twelve interactive chapters – from the 8th century to today's representation of leprechauns in films and in pop music. *Mon–Sat 9.30am–6.30pm, Sun 10.30am–6.30pm | adults 10, children from 3 years 8.50, under 3 years 3, family ticket 27 euro | 1 Jervis St. | www.leprechaunmuseum.ie | Luas: Jervis St.*

### CITY SAFARI

**VIKING SPLASH** (109 D6) *(Ø G5)*
On land and through water: this unusual city round trip has amphibious vehicles, which drive into the water and back out again. *Feb–Nov daily 10am, 11.30am, 2pm and 3.30pm | from St Stephen's Green | adults 20, children 10 euro | tel. 01 7 07 60 00 | www.vikingsplash.ie*

### BEACH & COAST

At the coastal village *Malahide* (117 E3) *(Ø 0)* there is a sandy beach, in *Killiney* (117 F5) *(Ø 0)* (p. 51) a nice pebble beach with a view over the Wicklow Mountains. Both beaches are quick to get to with the DART from Dublin's centre. And not far south of Killiney, on the coastal promenade in the small town of Bray (117 F6) *(Ø 0)*, is the *Aquarium National Sea Life Centre* with sharks, piranhas, seahorses and many other creatures *(Jan–March/Nov–Dec Mon–Fri 11am–5pm, Sat/Sun 10am–6pm, April–Oct daily 10am–6pm | admission adults 12, children 9, when booking online 7.50 and 6.50 euro respectively | 5 min on foot from the DART station Bray)*.

# FESTIVALS & EVENTS

All year round the Dubliners find occasions to have fun and the celebrations are of course led by their patron saint, St Patrick. Sports and culture also have their place on the calendar, but Ireland does not have big celebrations on religious holidays.

## PUBLIC HOLIDAYS

**1 Jan** *(New Year)*; **17 March** *(St Patrick's Day – National Day)*; **Easter Monday**; **also 1st Mon in May, June, Aug and last Mon in Oct** *(Bank Holiday)*; **25/26 Dec** *(Christmas)*. *Good Friday* is not an official public holiday, but the pubs are closed.

## EVENTS

### FEBRUARY

▶ *Dublin International Film Festival:* a week filled with Irish and international films: *tel. 01 6 62 42 60 | www.dubliniff.com*

### MARCH

▶ *St Patrick's Day:* Five days of carnival atmosphere with fairs, markets, music and dance with a massive parade in the city on the 17th. *www.stpatricksday.ie*

### APRIL

▶ *Messiah – 13 April:* Open air performance of George Frideric Handel's oratorio on Fishamble Street

### MAY

▶ *Africa Day – 25 May:* Music, food and lots of happenings – all about African culture: *www.africaday.ie*

### JUNE

▶ *Bloomsday – 16 June*: This is the day in 1904 that James Joyce's fiction 'Ulysses' takes place. Guided walks and events at the locations all pay homage to the work. Information: *The James Joyce Centre | tel. 01 8 78 85 47 | www.jamesjoyce.ie*
▶ *Dublin Writers Festival:* Readings and presentations of famous international authors; *mid-June, several days around Bloomsday | tel. 01 2 22 54 55 | www.dublin writersfestival.com*

### JUNE–AUGUST

▶ *Summer in Dublin:* Open air events including free midday concerts at Merrion Square and in other parks and more: *end June–mid-Aug | www.dublincity.ie*

**Everything goes green for St Patrick's Day but Dubliners celebrate more than their saint: beautiful horses, tough sports and literature**

## AUGUST

▶ *Dublin Horse Show:* On the grounds of the Royal Dublin Society (RDS) in the suburb of Ballsbridge. The Irish are horse lovers, but there is more to this than just an internationally acclaimed competition in show jumping.

▶ INSIDER TIP *Ladies' Day:* A social event, where you wear extravagant hats and there is also a large market fair that takes place around the main race track. *Wed–Sat of the 1st week in Aug | tickets tel. 0 81 83 00 20 74 | www.dublinhorse show.com*

## SEPTEMBER

▶ *Liffey Swim:* Since 1920 participants have swum the Liffey 2.5km/1.6mi downstream to a festival at Custom House.

▶ *Dublin Fringe Festival:* Theatre, dance, comedy and lots of cabaret are proof of the inexhaustible creativity of the Irish. *Two weeks mid-Sept | tel. 01 8 17 16 77 | www.fringefest.com*

▶● *Culture Night:* The big night of free culture – from A to Z, in the entire urban area. *www.culturenight.ie*

## SEPTEMBER/OCTOBER

▶ *Dublin Theatre Festival:* Contemporary theatre pieces from different countries are performed on the city's stages. *End Sept–mid-Oct. | tel. 01 6 77 88 99 | www. dublintheatrefestival.com*

## OCTOBER

▶ *Samhain/Halloween – 31 October*: Samhain is the Celtic name for Halloween, which thousands of costume-clad Dubliners celebrate with a parade from Parnell Square to Temple Bar.

▶ *Dublin Marathon:* Top class international athletes take part. *Last Mon in Oct | www.dublincitymarathon.ie*

# LINKS, BLOGS, APPS & MORE

LINKS

▶ www.visit-templebar.com Temple Bar Traders site includes all sorts of listings about events, markets, exhibitions, pubs and where to find the *craic*!

▶ www.storymap.ie Click on some of the speech bubbles on the city map and listen to the story. Locals like Seosamh O'Maolala (who tells a story about a

monster that gets up to mischief at the Royal Canal) or the actress Maureen Grant (who speaks about her wild times at the Olympia Theatre, where she went on a ghost hunt with Laurel and Hardy and cuddled with Kris Kristofferson) either way they are all very interesting. Most of the speech bubbles you can click on are situated in the south of the city

▶ www.designingdublin.com Designing Dublin's website has different categories like '100 exciting things you didn't know about the city centre' with 100 interesting sites or events. There is a neighbourhood guide and the heading 'Ask a local' where you can get advice from a local

▶ www.philpankov.com The Russian photographer Philip Pankov studied photography in Dublin and is considered Ireland's best traditional photographer. He works with a Hasselblad 501CM and he prints out his pictures in his own dark room. See his website for some of his best black and white photos of Dublin

BLOGS & FURUMS

▶ www.dublinblog.ie An excellent group blog – young writers and bloggers talk about their life in Dublin and the goings on with insight and humour

▶ totallydublin.ie/blog An informative resource about the cultural aspects of Dublin, especially with regard to films and music – also lots of videos. They promise to 'feature content on all facets of culture both Irish and international, music, film, fashion, bar and food reviews, and interviews'

**Regardless of whether you are still preparing your trip or already in Dublin: these addresses will provide you with more information, videos and networks to make your holiday even more enjoyable**

▶ www.nci.ie/ispy If you want to know what the weather is like in Dublin or if O'Shea's Pub is still open, have a look at this site with lots of live webcams in Dublin

▶ www.budgetplaces.com/dublin Here you will find dozens of videos about everyday life in the inner city, which give you an excellent idea of what to expect of Dublin. With the added bonus of lots of listings for inexpensive accommodation

▶ www.visitdublin.com/downloads/Dublin_Podcasts Dublin's Tourism Office has a series of free podcasts of audio guides that focus on different historical aspects of the city. There are twelve options to choose from each with maps and illustrations

▶ iGuide Dublin This is a mobile directory, each category leads you various important sites or places of interest in your immediate environment. The app also shows you the 'offer of the day' – a cheap restaurant, a special discount at a boutique, etc. – and the latest news in Dublin

▶ Spotted by Locals App Dublin Tips that you won't find in travel guides – hidden parks, café tips, unusual statues, flea markets, special city walks. Much of it is unknown even to local Dubliners

▶ www.lonelyplanet.com/thorntreeSearch?q=dublin The Thorntree Community shares experiences and useful tips in and around the Irish capital: what the best transport options are when you arrive, cheap accommodation suggestions and which restaurants are best avoided

▶ www.couchsurfing.org This site is popular with those tourists who are adventurous and who don't like to book in advance. Here, you will find a list of people who have a free bed or sofa and are more than happy to put guests up for the night. An excellent way to get to know the locals

# TRAVEL TIPS

## ARRIVAL

🚢 There are a number of ferry options for travel from Britain to Ireland. *Irish Ferries (www.irishferries.com)* operate daily between Holyhead and Dublin Port. *P & O Ferries (www.POferries.com)* operate daily between Liverpool and Dublin Port or there is a fast service between Holyhead and Dublin Port with *Stena Lines (www.stenaline.ie)* with a choice of either a Fast-craft or a Superferry.

✈ Most national airlines offer regular direct flights to Dublin Airport *(www.dublinairport.com)*. Ireland's national carrier *Aer Lingus (www.aerlingus.com)* also has regular flights from Britain and North America and Ryanair *(www.ryanair.com)* always has discounted fares. The airlines regularly offer specials so it is worth checking with your travel agent for cheap packages. *Aircoach* buses work around the clock, from 6am–8pm every 10 min

from the airport to the city. It takes about 40 minutes to get to the city centre on two routes: via O'Connell St., Grafton St., Kildare St., Leeson St. Lower to the suburbs of Sandyford and Leopardstown, and via O'Connell St., Grafton St. and Merrion Square to Ballsbridge. Single 8 euro, return 14 euro *(www.aircoach.ie)*. *Dublin Bus* is from 7am–11pm about every 10min, single 6 euro, return 10 euro, route 747 via O'Connell St. to the bus station (Busáras) **(109 E2)** *(〇 G4)*, 748 on the same route and further to Heuston Station. The drive to Busáras takes about 30 min **INSIDER TIP** for a tight budget: route 41/41C to Lower Abbey Street, single 2 euro, about 45 min.

🚆 There is also a train-ferry connection from London to Dublin. Connections inside Ireland: arrival from the north Connolly Station, from the south and west Heuston Station west of the city centre

## CAR HIRE

Dublin has the same kind of traffic as any international city and if you decide to drive then you need to consider if you want to arrive in the city by car or if you want rent one once there. You drive in the left lane in Ireland. The popular international car rentals are all at the airport. A local rental car company at the airport is *Irish Car Rentals | www.irishcarrentals.com | tel. 18 50 20 60 88*. If you have a flat tyre: *Automobile Association | tel. 016 17 99 99* or *RAC Motoring Service | tel. 1800 80 54 98*

## CLIMATE, WHEN TO GO

Dublin has a temperate climate (due to the influence of the Gulf Stream) and is

# From arrival to weather

**Holiday from start to finish: the most important addresses and information for your Dublin trip**

an all year round travel destination. Frost and snow seldom occur but it rains relatively consistently throughout the year. A good time to travel is in spring which starts in March, when the weather is mild. The sunniest and driest months are May and June with six hours of daily sunshine, but September and October can also be nice. But the temperature rarely gets higher than 25°C/77°F even in summer. Even in summer and you should be prepared for cold fronts on a daily basis, with constantly changing weather, so it is best to always pack warm clothing and rain gear.

## CONSULATES & EMBASSIES

**AMERICAN EMBASSY DUBLIN**
*42 Elgin Road | Ballsbridge | Dublin 4 | tel. +353 16 68 87 77 | dublin.usembassy.gov*

**BRITISH EMBASSY DUBLIN**
*29 Merrion Road | Ballsbridge | Dublin 4 | tel. +353 12 05 37 00 | britishembassyin ireland.fco.gov.uk/en*

## CUSTOMS

UK citizens do not have to pay any duty on goods brought from another EU country as long as tax was included in the price and are for private consumption. The limits are: 800 cigarettes, 400 cigarillo, 200 cigars, 1kg smoking tobacco,10L spirits, 20L liqueurs, 90L wine, 110L beer. Travellers from the USA, Canada, Australia or other non-EU countries are allowed to enter with the following tax-free amounts: 200 cigarettes or 100 cigarillos or 50 cigars or 250g smoking tobacco. 2L wine and spirits with less 22 vol % alcohol, 1L spirits with more than 22vol % alcohol content.

## CURRENCY CONVERTER

| £ | € | € | £ |
|---|---|---|---|
| 1 | 1.10 | 1 | 0.90 |
| 3 | 3.30 | 3 | 2.70 |
| 5 | 5.50 | 5 | 4.50 |
| 13 | 14.30 | 13 | 11.70 |
| 40 | 44 | 40 | 36 |
| 75 | 82.50 | 75 | 67.50 |
| 120 | 132 | 120 | 108 |
| 250 | 275 | 250 | 225 |
| 500 | 550 | 500 | 450 |

| $ | € | € | $ |
|---|---|---|---|
| 1 | 0.70 | 1 | 1.40 |
| 3 | 2.10 | 3 | 4.20 |
| 5 | 3.50 | 5 | 7 |
| 13 | 9.10 | 13 | 18.20 |
| 40 | 28 | 40 | 56 |
| 75 | 52.50 | 75 | 105 |
| 120 | 84 | 120 | 168 |
| 250 | 175 | 250 | 350 |
| 500 | 350 | 500 | 700 |

For current exchange rates see www.xe.com

Travellers to the US who are residents of the country do not have to pay duty on articles purchased overseas up to the value of $800, but there are limits on the amount of alcoholic beverages and tobacco products. For the regulations for international travel for US residents please see *www.cbp.gov*

## DUBLIN PASS

The *Dublin Pass* gives you free access to about 30 places of interest, free airport transfer with the Aircoach as well as various specials. You can get the pass online *(www.dublinpass.ie)* and in the *Dublin Tourism* offices, 35 euro for one, 55 for two, 65 for three and 95 for six days. Many attractions like the National Museum are free of charge anyway – it is INSIDERTIP worth it only for visitors that go to many sites, who can start using it from the airport to get to the city centre.

## ELECTRICITY

Voltage: 220 Volt. Irish electrical sockets are designed for three-pin plugs.

## EMERGENCY SERVICES

Police (Garda): *9 99* or *112*. This number is also valid for rescue services, the fire department and coastguard services.

## HEALTH

UK nationals and nationals with the European medical aid card (EHIC) can make use of the doctors and hospitals. The bill gets paid the same way as back home with the card. It is essential that

## BUDGETING

| | | |
|---|---|---|
| Guinness | £3.50/$5 | for a pint |
| Coffee | £2/$3.50 | per cup |
| Fish and chips | £5.50/$9 | for a portion |
| Bus ticket | £1.20–1.65/$2–2.50 | for a single fare |
| Music CD | £12/$20 | for Irish folk music |
| Theatre | £16/$25 | per ticket |

citizens from all other countries take out private medical insurance. You don't need to look far to find a pharmacy in Dublin. There are numerous pharmacies and *Boots* outlets.

## IMMIGRATION

Citizens of the UK, USA, Canada, Australia and New Zealand need only a valid passport to enter all countries of the EU. Children below the age of 12 need a children's passport.

## INFORMATION

### DUBLIN TOURISM
The tourism centre has several branches: *Airport Dublin* (117 E4) *(ω O)* | *Arrivals* | *daily 8am–10pm; main office: St Andrew's Church* (109 D4) *(ω G5)* | *Suffolk Street* | *Mon–Sat 9am–5.30pm, Sun 10.30am–3pm north of the Liffey: 14 O'Connell St. Upper* (112 C5) *(ω G4)* | *Mon–Sat 9am–5pm | tel. 353 18 50 23 03 30*

### TOURISM IRELAND UK
*103 Wigmore Street | London W1U 1QS | tel. +44 20 75 18 08 00 | www.discover ireland.com/gb*

### TOURISM IRELAND USA
*345 Park Avenue | New York, NY 10154 | tel. +1 212 418 08 00 | www.discoverireland. com/us*

## MONEY & CREDIT CARDS

The currency is the euro. ATMs for EC cards are available on almost every street corner in the city centre. The banks open Mon–Fri 10am–4pm, Thu until 5pm, and certain branches also open on Saturdays. Almost all credit cards are accepted in most of the shops, hotels and restaurants.

However, some private bed and breakfast establishments prefer to be paid in cash. Best ask when checking in!

## NEWSPAPERS

The most important daily newspapers in Dublin are the serious, liberal-minded *Irish Times,* the lighter, more conservative *Irish Independent* and the *Examiner.* The *Evening Herald* is an evening paper. You can also get English newspapers at most stores, some of which have Irish editions.

## OPENING HOURS

Business hours are generally Mon–Sat 9am–6pm but some do vary their closing times and have longer hours in the evening. Many shops are also open on Sundays afternoons. In the city centre most of the shops don't close before 8pm on Thursdays.

## PHONE & MOBILE PHONE

Using cell phones with GMS standard and roaming service in Ireland is hassle-free but expensive. So another option is to make use of **INSIDER TIP** certain designated public phones where overseas conversations only cost 0.25 euro per minute. Cheaper still are calls from **INSIDER TIP** call shops, of which the city centre has many. You can get phone cards for 10, 15 and 20 euro at the post office. Telephone directory: *118 50.* The dialling code for Ireland is *+353* and the area code is *(01)* for Dublin.

## POST

The Dublin post offices are open Mon–Fri from 9.30am–6pm, the General Post Office on O'Connell Street (109 D2) (*M G4*) from Mon–Sat 8am–8pm, Sun 10.30am–6.30pm.

## PUBLIC TRANSPORT

In Dublin's compact city centre many areas can be reached comfortably on foot. The train routes travel around the periphery of the city centre. There are numerous bus routes, but with the wide variety of different routes you need some help to get yourself orientated.

### BUSES

Buses stop on request. 'An Lar' on the destination indicates a bus that will take you to the city centre. There are a few different weekly tickets and multiple journey tickets, one of which is the *Rambler Ticket (p. 41).* They allow trips on all routes in the city district for 6 euro per person or 10.50 euro for a family ticket for an entire day. A combined bus–Luas ticket costs 7.50 euro per day, the bus/DART ticket 10.70 euro. Make sure **INSIDER TIP** you have enough change when taking the bus: as the drivers don't give change. Schedules and tickets: *Dublin Bus Office* (109 D2) (*M G4*) | 59 O'Connell St. Upper | tel. 01 8 73 42 22 | Mon–Sat 9am– 5.30pm | www.dublinbus.ie

### CYCLING 😊

Dublin is not the most bicycle-friendly city, the bicycle paths are not always separate but often consist of a brown line painted on to the street, and the car drivers are not very considerate. But bicycles are now also part of the public transport system as the city has adopted the practice, popular in many other European cities, of renting out bicycles. 450 robust bicycles are available at 40 stations in the city centre; the individual stations are at the most 300m apart from each other. In order to rent a bike, you have to become a member and for tourists it is worth getting the 3-day membership for 2 euro. You can pay at 14 of the 40 stations with your credit card.

The membership ID carries a PIN number which you will need when taking a bicycle. The first 30 min are free. Afterwards it costs 50c per hour, 1.50 for two hours, 3.50 for three hours and 6.50 for four hours and 2 euro for every following half hour. You can find information about the bike sharing scheme and the stations at *www.dublinbikes.ie*.

### DART

Dublin Area Rapid Transport (DART) is the rail line that connects the northern and southern suburbs and coastal regions with the inner city – Connolly Station north of the Liffey, Tara Street and Pearse Street in the south. For ● trips to the coast and for Dublin visitors with accommodation near the DART stations, it is really convenient *(every 10–15 min from 6am– midnight | www.irishrail.ie)*. The day ticket for 7.60 euro is worth it after four rides. For trips it is recommendable to get a return ticket at a vending machine or ticket counter.

### ECOCABS ☺ ●

Strong cyclists will take you to any destination within Dublin's city centre in modern, covered tricycles, also in a radius of about 2km/1.2mi around the O'Connell Bridge. They ride between 10am and 7pm and have certain stops, but can also be waved down. They are sponsored by companies, so you don't need to pay them, but a tip will be greatly appreciated. Don't mistake the Ecocabs with the rickshaws or bicycle taxis that demand a fee! *www.ecocabs.ie*

# WEATHER IN DUBLIN

| | Jan | Feb | March | April | May | June | July | Aug | Sept | Oct | Nov | Dec |
|---|---|---|---|---|---|---|---|---|---|---|---|---|
| **Daytime temperatures in °C/°F** | | | | | | | | | | | | |
| | 8/46 | 8/46 | 10/50 | 12/54 | 15/59 | 18/64 | 20/68 | 19/66 | 17/63 | 14/57 | 10/50 | 8/46 |
| **Nighttime temperatures in °C/°F** | | | | | | | | | | | | |
| | 2/36 | 2/36 | 2/36 | 3/37 | 6/43 | 9/48 | 11/52 | 10/50 | 9/48 | 6/43 | 3/37 | 2/36 |
| **Sunshine hours/day** | | | | | | | | | | | | |
| | 2 | 3 | 4 | 6 | 7 | 7 | 6 | 5 | 4 | 3 | 2 | 2 |
| **Precipitation days/month** | | | | | | | | | | | | |
| | 13 | 11 | 10 | 11 | 11 | 11 | 13 | 13 | 12 | 12 | 12 | 13 |
| **Water temperatures in °C/°F** | | | | | | | | | | | | |
| | 9/48 | 8/46 | 7/45 | 8/46 | 9/48 | 11/52 | 13/55 | 14/57 | 14/57 | 13/55 | 12/54 | 10/50 |

## LUAS

The fast and modern commuter rail, Luas, rides on two routes. The red route takes you from Connolly Station parallel to the Liffey on the northern bank almost up to Phoenix Park, crosses over the river to Heuston Station and then to the south-west suburbs. The green route, on the other hand, connects the southern suburbs of Dublin with St Stephen's Green *(every 10 min or more frequently from 5.30am–0.30am, Sat from 6.30am, Sun from 7am | www.luas.ie)*. You can get tickets at a vending machine and in shops near the stops.

## SIGHTSEEING TOURS

There are a number of good walking tours for the Dublin visitor. A favourite is the ● *Literary Pub Crawl*. Two actors lead you through the pubs and entertain you with pieces of Samuel Beckett, Oscar Wilde and company. *(April–Oct daily, Nov–March Thu–Sat 7.30pm, starting at the pub The Duke | Duke St. | www.dublinpubcrawl.com | tel. 01 6 70 56 02)*. With the brochure *Rock 'n' Stroll Trail (at the Tourist Office)* music lovers will find where stars like U2 lived and worked. You can also view Dublin from the Liffey: boat trips start at the northern bank *(Bachelors Walk)* near Ha'penny Bridge *(March–Nov four to six times daily about 45 min for 13 euro | tel. 01 4 73 40 82 | www.liffeyvoyage.ie)*.

You can also quite literally get a taste of Dublin: with the INSIDER TIP *Dublin Tasting Trail* which mixes sightseeing with culinary pleasures. The 2.5 hour tour takes you to markets, fish shops, bakeries, butcheries and cheese shops, some of which have been in one family for four to five generations. And best of all: at each one of the many stops you can have a taste test. The tour starts at 10am on Fridays and Saturdays depending on the route at the various points in the centre *(45 euro | tel. 014 97 12 45 | www.fabfoodtrails.com/dublin-tasting-trail)*.

## TAXI

Since the Irish government has awarded far more taxi licences, it is no longer a problem to get a taxi even on weekends. You can get a taxi in the city centre at College Green, at Aston Quay and on O'Connell Street. The basic fee is 3.80 euro during the day and 4.10 euro at night for the first kilometre. Every following kilometre costs 0.95–1.63 euro depending on the distance. For the drive from the airport to the city you can expect to pay 25–30 euro. There are sufficient taxis, but when it is important to be on time (for example when going to the airport) you should order a taxi beforehand *(e.g. A to B Cabs | tel. 01 6 77 22 22; Castle Cabs | tel. 01 8 31 90 00; Checkers Cabs | tel. 01 8 34 34 34; Pony Cabs | 01 6 61 22 33)*.

## TIPPING

10–15 per cent is the norm for a tip at a restaurant, but that is only if an amount has not already been added as a service charge, 10 per cent of the cost of the ride is a standard tip for a taxi driver. As a rule no tip is given in pubs if you fetch your drink at the counter but if you are served at a table, you should tip.

## TIME

The time in Ireland in summer is Greenwich Mean Time (GMT) +1 and in winter the time is shifted back one hour to GMT.

## WEIGHTS & MEASURES

The Metric System is used in Ireland with one exception: draft beer in the pubs is in pints.

# NOTES

# MARCO POLO TRAVEL GUIDES

**MARCO POLO**
With ROAD ATLAS & PULL-OUT MAP
**FRENCH RIVIERA**
NICE, CANNES & MONACO
SPECTACULAR GRAND CANYON DU VERDON
Breath-taking scenery that takes some beating
SNIFFING THE AIR
The perfume manufacturers of Grasse
Travel with **Insider Tips**
www.marco-polo.com

**MARCO POLO**
With STREET ATLAS & PULL-OUT MAP
**NEW YORK**
MEADOWS, WILD FLOWERS AND SKYSCRAPERS
Green is chic- the High Line in Chelsea
COCKTAIL ON CLOUD NINE
Rooftop bar at 230 Fifth Street
Travel with **Insider Tips**

**MARCO POLO**
**AKE GARDA**
NTE BALDO WITH MOUNTAIN BIKE
ine car in Malcesine takes bikes too
"KISSES" IN SALÒ
chocolate „baceri"
Travel with **Insider Tips**

**MARCO POLO**
With ROAD ATLAS & PULL-OUT MAP
**ALLORCA**
AN FLAIR IN THE MEDITERRANEAN
Mallorca's most beautiful beach
„IN" CROWD MEET
vida in Deià
Travel with **Insider Tips**

**MARCO POLO**
With STREET ATLAS & PULL-OUT MAP
**BERLIN**
A STUNNING ISLAND JUST FOR ART
...using treasures from around the world
COOL AT NIGHT
tin club scene sets the trend
Travel with **Insider Tips**

- PACKED WITH INSIDER TIPS
- BEST WALKS AND TOURS
- FULL-COLOUR PULL-OUT MAP
  AND STREET ATLAS

# STREET ATLAS

The green line ▬▬ indicates the Walking tours (p. 86–91)

All tours are also marked on the pull-out map

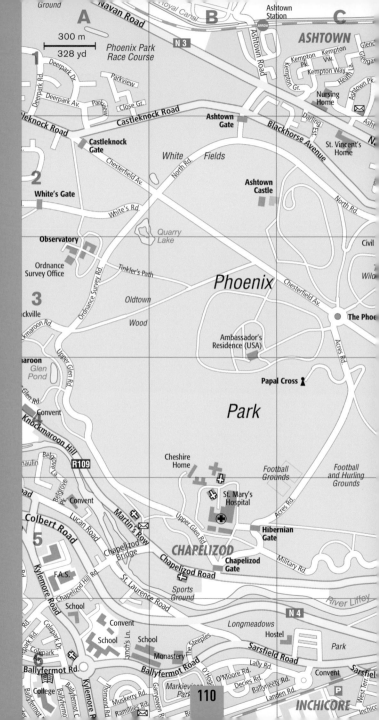

Ground

Navan Road

Royal Canal

Ashtown
Station

B

ASHTOWN

C

N 3

300 m

328 yd

Phoenix Park
Race Course

Deerpark Rd.

Deerpark Dr.

Parkview

Deerpark Av.

Parkview

Close Gr.

Kempton
Pk.

Kempton
Gr.

Glenc

Glenga

Kempton Way

Kempton Pk.

Heath

Ashtown Pk.

Ashtown Rd.

Nursing
Home

Ashtown

1

leknock Road

Castleknock Road

Ashtown
Gate

Blackhorse Avenue

Darling

St. Vincent's
Home

N

Castleknock
Gate

Chesterfield Av.

White

Fields

North Rd.

Ashtown
Castle

White's Gate

White's Rd.

North Rd.

2

Observatory

Quarry
Lake

Civil

Ordnance
Survey Office

Tinkler's Path

Phoenix

Chesterfield Av.

Wilo

ckville

Ordnance Survey Rd.

Oldtown

3

kmaroon Rd.

Wood

The Phoe

maroon

Upper Glen Rd.

Ambassador's
Residence (USA)

Glen
Pond

Acres Rd.

Glen Rd.

Papal Cross

Convent

Park

Knockmaroon Hill

R109

naulin

BelGrove La.

Cheshire
Home

Football
Grounds

Football
and Hurling
Grounds

Convent

Belgrove

Lucan Road

Martin's Row

St. Mary's
Hospital

Acres Rd.

Colbert Road

5

ad

Chapelizod
Bridge

Chapelizod Hill Rd.

Chapelizod Road

CHAPELIZOD

Upper Glen Rd.

Hibernian
Gate

Military Rd.

Kylemore Road

F.A.S.

St. Laurence Road

Chapelizod
Gate

School

Sports
Ground

River Liffey

Convent

Longmeadows

N 4

Park

School

School

Lynch's Ln.

School

The Steeples

Hostel

Sarsfield Road

Convent

P

k Rd.

Colpark Dr.

Colpark

Monastery

Lally Rd.

Sarsfie

College

Ballyfermot Rd.

Ballyfermot Road

O'Hoga

O'Moore Rd.

Decies Rd.

Ballyneety Rd.

Landen Rd.

West Ter

Inchic

Kylemore R

Ballyfermot C

Muskerry Rd.

Garryowen Rd.

Ramillies Rd.

Marklevieson
Park

110

INCHICORE

**D**

Ashington Pk.
Priory N.
Priory W.
Priory E.
Kinvara Av.
Abbey Dr.
Church Wlk.
Schools
Sports Ground
Park Gdns.
Villa Park Rd.
Villa
Villa Park Av.
Nephin Road
Blackhorse Avenue
an Gate
North Rd.

Áras an Uachtaráin
dence of the
dent of Ireland)

Polo Rd.
Chesterfield Av.
Pavillion
Polo Ground

Athletic
ound

Citadel Pond
Cricket Ground

Thomas Hill

Islandbridge Gate
Military Rd.
Chapelizod Road

DGE

University Boat House

n National
emorial Park
Hurling Grounds

Con Colbert Road

Inchicore Road
Kilmainham Gaol/Jail
Richmond
Park
mmoc River
Emmet Road
ugh
Sq.
St. Michael's
Church
Bulfin Rd.

**E**

Ballyboggan Road
Royal Canal
Lagan Rd.
Boyne Rd.
Nore Rd.
Ratoath Road
Ashington Dr.
Dominican Convent
Carnlough Rd.
Bannow Rd.
Broombridge Rd.
Killala Rd.
School
Kilkieran Rd.
Liscannor Rd.
Faussagh Road
Dingle
Pope John Paul II Park
Apostolic Nunciature
Nephin Road
Croagh-patrick Rd.
St. Joseph's School
Ratoath Road
Navan Road
Skreen Road
Slemish Rd.
Dunard Av.
Dunard Rd.
Military Cemetery
Dunard Dr.
Employment Exchange
Glenbeigh Rd.
Glenbeigh Pk.
Fish Pond
Spa Rd.
McKee Dr.
North Rd.
Blackhorse Avenue
Zoo Rd.
McKee Barracks
Zoological Gardens
Garda Siochána H.Q.
Fountain Rd.
People's Garden
Aberdeen
Gough Monument
Cricket Ground
Army Athletic Ground
Chesterfield Av.
Department of Defence
Wellington Monument
Park Gate
Wellington Rd.
Conyngham Road
R109
Sarah Bridge
South Circular Road
Clancy Barracks
School
St. John's Road West
Irish Museum of Modern Art (Royal Hospital)
KILMAINHAM
Courth House
Kilmainham Ln.
Old Kilmainham
Mount Brown
Cameron
Donelan Av.
R111
School
South

**111**

**F**

Pidgeon
Slaney Cl.
Slaney Rd.
Blackwater Rd.
Barrow Rd.
Lee Rd.
Moyle Rd.
Broombridge Station
St. Finbar's Rd.
School
Muroy Rd.
Carnlough Rd.
Bannow Rd.
St. Attraa Rd.
St. Fintan
St. Jarla
St. Finbar's Clubhouse
CABRA
Quarry Road
Eris Rd.
Leix
Cabra Road
N 3
Old Cabra Road
Cabra Dr.
Cabra House
Annamoe
Ellesmere Av.
Black-horse Gr.
Drumalee Rd.
Prussia Street
Hall
Aughrim Street
Ben Adar Rd.
Oxmantown Rd.
Arbow St.
Arklow St.
Halliday Rd.
O'Devaney Gdns.
Montpellier Mews
St. Bricin's Military Hospital
Montpellier Gdns.
St. Bricin's Pk.
Arbour Hill Prison
National Museum of Ireland (Collins Barracks)
Montpellier Hill
Parkgate Street
Wolfe To
N 4
Heuston Station
Garda
Victoria
Heuston
Technical Bureau
Steeven's Hospital
St. James's Brew (Guinn)
Military Rd.
St. Patrick's Hospital
Bow Ln. W.
James's Street
James's
Bow Br.
Ewington Ln.
Gr. James's Pl.
Guinn Storeho
St. James's Hospital
School
Bassin St. Lwr.

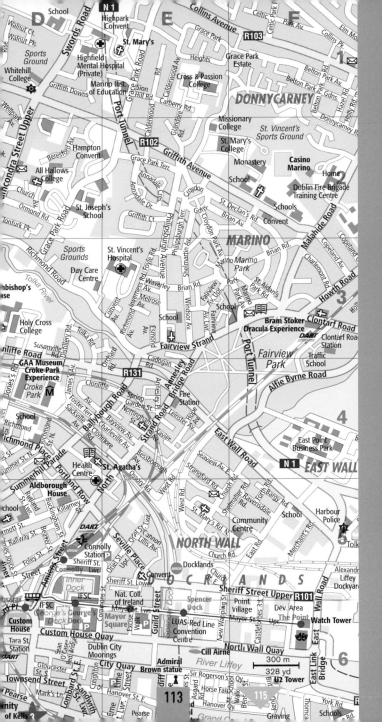

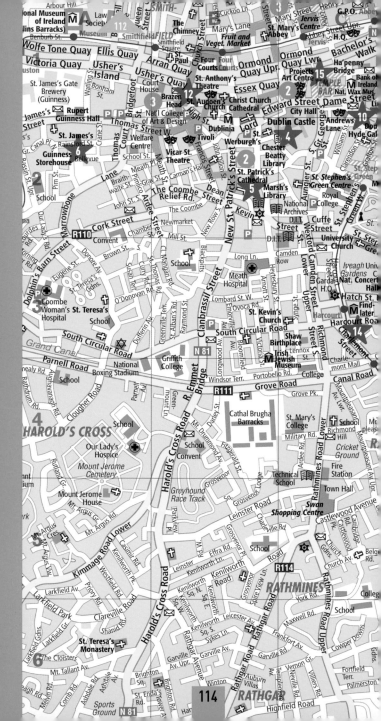

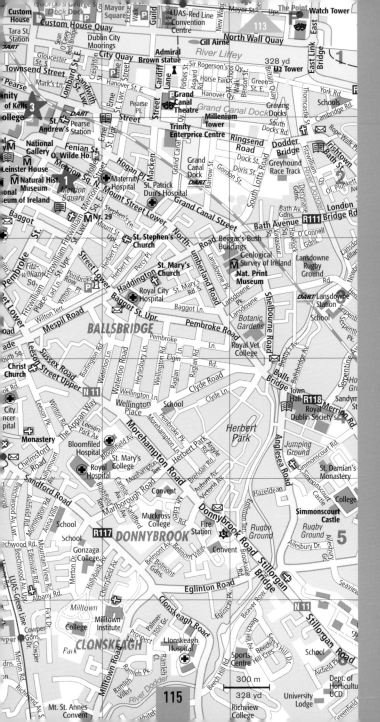

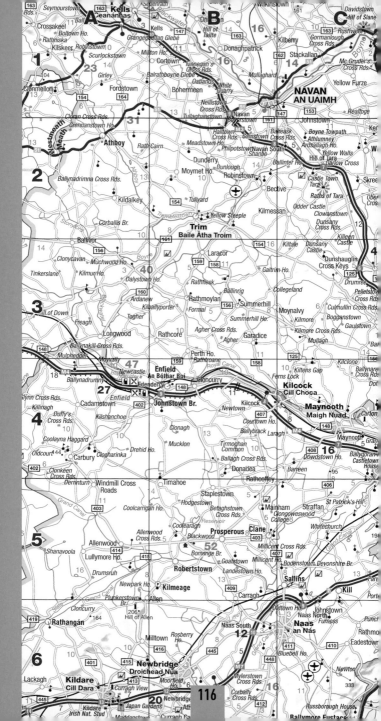

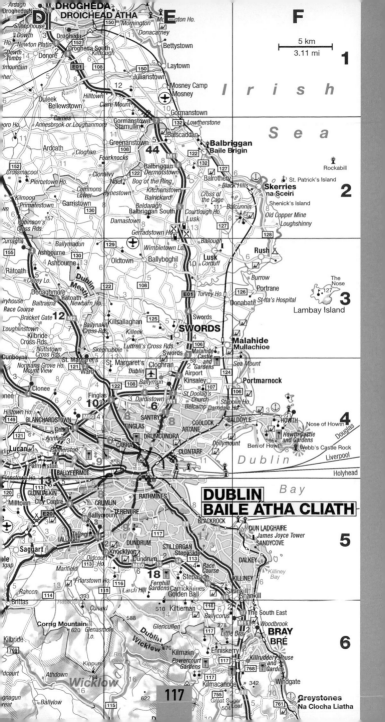

This index lists a selection of the streets and squares shown in the street atlas

# KEY TO STREET ATLAS

| | |
|---|---|
| 𝕄 | Museum |
| 🎭 | Stage / Bühne |
| ℹ | Information |
| ♱ | Church / Kirche |
| ✡ | Synagogue / Synagoge |
| ✚ | Hospital / Krankenhaus |
| ✿ | Police / Polizei |
| ✉ | Post |
| 📖 | Library / Bibliothek |
| ♟ | Monument / Denkmal |
| ❋ | Botanic garden / Botanischer Garten |
| 🐘 | Zoo |
| P | Parking / Parkplatz |
| ⚠ | Youth Hostel / Jugendherberge |
| ─●─ | Tram with station / Tram mit Station |
| *DART* | Dublin Area Rapid Transit |
| ⬛ | Remarkable building / Bemerkenswertes Gebäude |
| ⬛ | Public building / Öffentliches Gebäude |
| ⬜ | Green / Grünfläche |
| ⬜ | Uncovered area / Unbebaute Fläche |
| ▨▨▨ | Pedestrian zone / Fußgängerzone |
| ▬▬ | Walking tours / Stadtspaziergänge |
| ★1 | MARCO POLO Highlight |

# INDEX

This index lists all sights, museums, and destinations, plus the names of important people and key words featured in this guide. Numbers in bold indicate a main entry.

# WRITE TO US

e-mail: info@marcopologuides.co.uk

Did you have a great holiday?
Is there something on your mind?
Whatever it is, let us know!
Whether you want to praise, alert us
to errors or give us a personal tip –
MARCO POLO would be pleased to
hear from you.
We do everything we can to provide the
very latest information for your trip.

Nevertheless, despite all of our authors'
thorough research, errors can creep in.
MARCO POLO does not accept any
liability for this. Please contact us by
e-mail or post.

MARCO POLO Travel Publishing Ltd
Pinewood, Chineham Business Park
Crockford Lane, Chineham
Basingstoke, Hampshire RG24 8AL
United Kingdom

**PICTURE CREDITS**
Cover ph...
W. Die...
51, 52,...
89); E...
(1 top),...
2 centr...
Axiom...
(17 bot...
Transg...

**1st Edi...**
World...
Crockf...
© MA...
Chief e...
Author...
Progra...
Picture...
What's...
Cartog...
Cartog...
Transla...
Prepres...
All righ...
or by a...
the pub...
Printed in Germany on non-chlorine bleached paper

# DOS & DON'TS 👆

**A few things to look out for in Dublin**

## DO ORDER A ROUND

In the pubs in Ireland ordering a round is the norm. So if you have made some new friends with Irish locals and join them in the pub they will certainly always buy the first round. That means that the next round is on you. Don't wait until your own glass is empty before you order the round: the speed of the next round depends on the fastest drinker.

## DON'T DRESS INAPPROPRIATELY

If your plans include going out to a good restaurant for dinner, drinking in a stylish cocktail bar or dancing in an exclusive club, you will need to pack something better than running shoes and jeans. If you dress too casually you may feel awkward or worst still: you will be barred from entering by the bouncer.

## DON'T SMOKE IN ENCLOSED PUBLIC AREAS

In Dublin smoking is not allowed in all pubs, restaurants, public transport or other public spaces. Many guesthouses have consequently created smoking areas on terraces or at their entrance area. The smoking laws are strictly adhered to and have some positive consequences and you may find that the air you breathe in the pubs is better than in front of the door.

## DO TRY NOT TO COMPLAIN ABOUT COUNTRY AND FOLK

The Irish like to complain about prices, the traffic and other difficulties in their country. They are allowed to. But as a guest you should not agree with them when they complain about these annoyances, whether it is about the litter on the streets, or about the lack of bread options at the bakery. You won't be very popular, even if the Irish nod in agreement out of politeness.

## DO LOOK RIGHT FIRST

The Irish drive on the left. And the stress-free days for drivers and pedestrians are also a thing of the past in Dublin. One look in the wrong direction can be a question of life or death as buses, cars and trucks thunder through the streets from early until late.

## DO AVOID POLITICS AND RELIGION

Ireland has a complex social history and unless you are invited by a local to discuss politics, the peace process, religion or work then it is best not to comment. These issues are still controversial and best avoided unless you know the people very well.